# THE BEST Little COOKBOOK IN THE WEST

Compiled and written by Loaun Werner Vaad

Illustrations and cartoons by Laura Karlen

# The Best Little Cookbook In The West

Published by:
Loaun Werner Vaad
HC 69, Box 210
Chamberlain, SD 57325
605-734-5135

Library Of Congress Catalog Number:
96-90358

ISBN: 0-9652586-2-9

Illustrations and cartoons by
Laura Karlen, Box 1346, Reliance, SD 57569

Vol. 1, First, Second and Third Printings at
Register-Lakota Printing, Chamberlain, SD 57325

Other books available:
A Taste Of Prairie Life

*Whoa there!* Rein in those horses at the next wide spot in the road. It's time for a chuckle or two and some reminiscing over the "*Good Old Days*". Got some kindling along? Get the campfire lit, and stir up some vittles.

Try something original like Jerry's Oyster-Oyster Stew. (He was not allowed to put in his pancake recipe. Jerry doesn't even get to <u>make</u> pancakes anymore!) There are favorites of family and friends, but you will also find recipes collected by cowpokes and stolen by desperados.

If you're looking for a new dish to serve, a remedy for that "pain in the neck" or just want to do some reminiscing, spend some time reading **The Best Little Cookbook In The West.**

*Happy Trails and Good Eating,*
*Loaun*

# Dedication

*The Best Little Cookbook In The West is dedicated to all those who won or tried to win the West; to name a few:*

John DeSmet, Meriwether Lewis, Hilda Isburg, Nels Larson, David Frame, William Clark, Rattlesnake Pete, Sam Abdnor, Sacajawea, Grover Boling, Loyd Harless, Ole Schervem, Kitty LeRoy, Selah Chamberlain, Mary Wier, A.P. Dixon, Bertha Dierks, Wild Bill Hickok, George McManus, Grant Anderson, Ozitte Lindley, W.P. Lyman, Theodore Roosevelt, Chief Drifting Goose, W.E. Roeser, Rocky Mountain Tom, Gov. M.Q. Sharpe, Will Andera, Esther Ellis, Carrie Larsen, John Bess, Judge John J. Bartine, Myrtle Wiard, Gilbert Crazy Bull, Albert Mueller, Mrs. E.A. Barlow, Anna Fasbender, Gilbert Wiard, Dr. Allcott, Fred Nissen, Jesse James, Hilda Fors, Mary Stocks, Anton Struka, Joe Hickey, Frank Bunker, B.G. Watson, Dan Grassrope, Ed Schooler, Robert Audiss, A.C. Miller, Olaf Nelson, Chief Black Kettle, Gottlieb Reuer, Joe Knippling, Ed Werner, George Custer, Ira Moffitt, Harry Holmes, Andrew Christensen, Emil Anderson, Julius Hass, Ernest Krause, A. Brakke, Dorothy Schrieber, Olaf Nelson, Newt Downs, Leona Hickey, Pete Murray, Gertrude McAnaly, Frank Malach, John Woster, Buffalo Calf Robe Woman, Horace Wagner, August Erickson, Ben Brave, Simon Audiss, Emil Parkening, Ed Lippens, Alex Booher, Merrill Karlen, Sr., Daniel Iron Nest, Olaf Erickson, Stanley Millan, Joe Morrissey, Andrew Lien, Wilmer Green, Joe Bice, William Schooler, Amy Carpenter, Ora Forell, Nettie Cosgrove, Baman Strong, Crazy Horse, Frank Vaad, W.H.H. Beadle, Roy Audiss, A.P. Long, William Williamson, Arthur Schmitt, Edythe Hickey, John Wheeler, Frank Scheffer, Fannie Garretson, Jack McCall, Ed Counselor, Kitty LeRoy, Joe Two Hawks, Blanche Luge, Frank Smith, Fred Fletcher, William Dinehart, Fannie Garretson, Elwood Kentsch, John B. Jones, Jacob Dierks, Rev. Henry Smith, Joshua Blare, Edna Butcher, Joseph Langdeau, Chris Hellekson, Fred Kenobbie, Bill Audiss, Roscoe Dean, Frank Bartlett, William Royal Ellis, Minor Wiard, Harry Mills, Howard Ellis, Morris Shrake, Reuben Wiard, Minnie Wiedman, Amanda Audiss, Herman Fritz, Henry Gregory, Chief Iron Nation, Henry Lein, Sidney Hockersmith, Judge Swift Hawk, Erick Hade, I. Rockefellow, Charlie Lyons, Frank Hall, Enoch Halverson, Jackson King, Charles Pease......

# Foreword

Cottonwood trees with old hanging ropes, dusty wagon trails, buffalo grazing on the prairie, wild horses running free over the rolling hills, deer making trails in lush grasses as they walk single file to water, and *blue sky*—such was the plains area of the west in the 1800's.

Things change and yet they stay the same. The prairies are still dotted with cottonwood trees, but the ropes are children's swings. The dusty trails are gravel roads leading off of the paved highways. There are still buffalo, but cattle are seen in more abundance. Most of the horses running free have gotten away from the cowhand that's wanting to saddle up! The deer walk single file to water, but you'll see them jumping barbwire fences. It's the late 1900's and when you look up it's so blue you know you're looking right into heaven. But, there again, that's not the same as when the banker says it looks like a whole lot of *"blue sky"*!

Loaun Werner was born and raised under that blue sky in the great plains area of the west. She makes the prairies her home with her husband, Jerry Vaad. They have two children, Tracy and Travis. Jerry and Loaun have a small ranch in addition to his work in the recreation department at St. Joseph's Indian School and her framing and art business.

Tracy owns and operates a gift shop business plus the decorative pheasant feather wreath business started by Loaun. Travis has worked as a counselor and recently returned to SD from Nashville, Tennessee. He is pursuing a songwriting career in the gospel and country music field.

LAURA KARLEN: THE BOOK'S ILLUSTRATOR HAS SPENT MOST OF HER LIFE SURROUNDED BY TALENTED COWBOYS, FARMERS, AND COOKS. MANY OF THE BOOKS PICTURES ARE 'DRAWN' FROM WITNESSED EVENTS. (NOTE: EVEN THE MOST TALENTED-HARDWORKING-ATTRACTIVE-SKILLED PROFESSIONALS HAVE HAD LAUGHABLE DAYS)(CNOT INTENTIONALLY)) (((MAYBE NOT A DAY; MAYBE JUST A LAUGHABLE NANO-SECOND)))

TAKE THAT BACK, THE ILLUSTRATOR HASN'T SEEN ANYTHING WHAT-SO-EVER LIKE WHAT'S PICTURED IN THIS BOOK. NOTHING; I WAS... SHE WAS..MISQUOTED.

ANYWAY...AS FAR AS RECIPES FOR THE COOKBOOK, THE ARTIST HAS JUST ONE 'RELIABLE' RECIPE.

## LAURA'S DRIVE THROUGH BURGER

YOU'LL NEED:

CASH      A VOICE
ONE CAR    A FAST FOOD RESTAURANT

1. DRIVE ALREADY FUELED CAR INTO A WELL-TRAVELED FAST FOOD OBSTACLE COURSE.

2. UPON REACHING A TALKING/LISTENING SIGN; CLEARLY STATE: "I WANT A HAMBURGER." (NOTE: SOME ESTABLISHMENTS GIVE NICK NAMES TO THEIR SANDWICHES. YOU MAY NEED AN INTERPRETER.)

3. DRIVE UP TO A SMALL WINDOW PRO-TRUDING FROM THE ESTABLISHMENT.

4. EXCHANGE CASH FOR BURGER.

5. BON APPETITE.

# WANTED*

### Open Faced Bean Sandwich
*(Open face, insert sandwich, bean sandwich)*

**8 ounce can pork 'n beans**
**8 strips bacon, already fried (can be left over from breakfast)**
**4 slices cheese**
**4 slices toast**
**Catsup, optional**
**Margarine, optional**

Lightly spread toast slices with margarine (optional). Arrange toast slices on cookie sheet. Place two slices of bacon on each slice toast. Layer bacon with desired amount of beans (people's appetites and tolerances vary). Top with cheese. Broil in oven until cheese melts. Serve with or without catsup. **Serves 2 to 4 people or 1 point rider.**

*Recipe from our illustrator, Laura Karlen.

## In Control

I fear horses. They intimidate me and leave me vulnerable to not being in control. Understand this. I like being in control.

Having a horse was a wish of us girls. Dad obliged. Now, we didn't need a horse as our pastures were flat. Pickups and feet were used to round up cattle.

It began when I was ten. Excited about the adventure, I paced impatiently as Dad saddled the horse and made the necessary adjustments. The ride was going to be from the barn to the end of our lane - 500 feet. What fun! As I reined the horse around for the return trip, control went from my court to his. He raced back to the comfort of his barn dwelling. Not only seeing the scenery flash by in a blur but also losing five pounds by chiseling away skin and bone on a saddle horn are both unnerving and painful!

Horses did not exit my life. I married a West River rancher. Convincing me about the gentleness of his favorite horse Puny was not easy. Would I willingly give control of my life to an equine one more time? This scenario was less traumatic, but one fact was confirmed: I fear horses.

Rejoicing over children who finally had legs long enough to reach the stirrups, I could remove myself from the world of horses.

"Mom, come quickly! Hold our horses! Dad is ready to go!" They were kidding, right? Hold TWO horses at ONE time? Why would these children think that it was so important to use the convenience of a house bathroom when they were going to be riding on the open prairie where bathrooms abound by every blade of grass? As they dismount and rush into the house, I realize those horses are not going to stand unattended very long. Will I be dragged unmercifully across the yard and into the pasture? Will my arms be dislocated from the joints? Cautiously reaching for the loose reins, I detect looks of compassion in those big brown eyes. The message seemed to be, "Why are you shaking? We will not harm you." Gloria, do not be fooled! "Thanks, Mom; see you later." Phew! Task completed without incident.

When our daughter was old enough for 4-H, her love for horses led her to the project space entitled "Horse." Confidently she placed her X. On the day of the county 4-H show I aged ten years. Jim's schedule always seemed booked with work. My only responsibility was to drive the pickup that pulled the horse trailer with the horse. Sitting beside me on the seat was a little girl wearing a big smile. Why couldn't I recognize her same enthusiasm? "Mom, everything will be okay; Babe and I get along fine. Don't worry." Don't worry? If that huge (looked huge to me) horse made one misstep, what would happen to my little girl? "What if somebody spooks Babe?" I asked. "Mom, I am in control." How could this little girl be in control when I wasn't?

During one county show intense heat shared the day. All of a sudden I saw the judge run toward Tonya. "What had that horse done to her?" I queried. She had locked her knees thus creating a fainting spell. The horse? He stood gently by as he watched his owner and friend being carried from the arena. They truly were companions. No, there was no need for Mom to worry.

If you qualify at the county 4-H horse show, you earn the right to compete at the State 4-H Horse Show. Eleven miles from home with this pickup, horse trailer, and horse is one thing. 120 miles? No way! Assuming the role of an in-control Mom, I schemed, "Tonya, if you leave your horse home, you can still compete with the horse quiz bowl team, and we can stay overnight so that you can watch some of the other events." Hesitantly she agreed. She also shared compassion for a mom with a fear of horses even though she could not understand it. The horse? With this decision control was again in his court. South Dakota temperatures during the State 4-H Horse Show usually soar into the 100+. Standing in the shade of the barn, I can see the smile on the horse's face!

With the advent of the four wheelers Jim began to use horses less and less. Where are the big brown eyes that looked at me empathetically and inferred, "Don't be afraid; we won't hurt you"?

~~~~~~~~~~~~~~~~~~~~~~~~~~~~~~~~~~~~~

Gloria Schaefer is the owner of Dynamics for Excellence headquartered north of Kennebec, South Dakota. She researches and develops selected presentations for any organization or business. Her enthusiastic, professional style is shared through messages of inspiration, motivation, education, and patriotism. Gloria taught 23 years and continues to ranch with her husband Jim. To enhance your next meeting, call 605-869-2357.

# Table of Contents

*continued*

*continued*

Got room for more vittles in your cellar? You may want to "store up" to make it through those long prairie winters.

Now your favorite pet might take offense at the names of some of our recipes, so we've included several treats to soothe <u>their</u> appetites, too!

Old and new remedies to help heal the body, mind and spirit! Plus other "stuff"...........

# CHUCKWAGON CHOW

# WANTED

*Barbecue and Ranch House Style Recipes*

CHUCKWAGON →
ORGANIZER

MANY CHUCKWAGONS WERE
EQUIPPED WITH A BACK CUPBOARD.
THIS GAVE THE COOK EASY
ACCESS TO TOOLS & INGREDIENTS;
KEPT ITEMS CLEANER; AND
PREVENTED THE CONTENTS FROM
BECOMING INTERMIXED....

...THAT WAS
LEFT TO THE
PROFESSIONALS.

## Three Bean Chili

A hearty recipe for the cowboy who thinks chili means "beans"!

**1 1/2 pounds ground beef**
**2 cups celery, chopped**
**1 large onion, chopped**
**3 garlic cloves, thin sliced**
**1 can kidney beans**
**1 can pinto beans**
**1 can refried beans**
**7 ounce can chopped green chilies**
**2 cans tomato soup**
**2 cups tomato juice***
**1 teaspoon salt**
**1/2 teaspoon black pepper**
**3 to 4 tablespoons chili powder**
**Water**

Brown the ground beef. Add celery, onion and garlic, cooking until they start to get soft. Remove as much fat as possible. Add remaining ingredients. Add water to make the chili the consistency you like. This is best if slow simmered for at least an hour. Serves six hungry people or a couple of cowhands.

Note: Jerry is our chili maker. He likes to substitute stewed tomatoes for the juice to give more texture to the chili.

PINTO        PAINT        APPALOOSA
BEAN         BEAN           BEAN

## Bandito Breakfast Burritos

**10 to 12 count package flour tortillas**
**1 pound sausage, bulk**
**1 medium onion, chopped**
**8 to 10 eggs, beaten**
**2 cups shredded cheese**

Sprinkle tortillas with water. Stack and seal in foil. Warm in 325 degree oven. Cook sausage with onion until sausage is crumbly. Remove sausage. Stir eggs into drippings and cook until set, stirring frequently. Add sausage. Spoon onto tortillas. Sprinkle with cheese. Roll tortillas. Serve with picante sauce or salsa.

## Donna's 26 Bar Ranch Eggs

**4 ounce can green chilies**
**1 pound Monterey Jack cheese**
**1 pound sharp cheddar cheese**
**4 eggs, separated**
**1 tablespoon flour**
**2/3 cup evaporated milk**
**1 teaspoon salt**
**Pinch of pepper**
**2 tomatoes**

Put half of chilies in bottom of buttered glass rectangular baking dish. Place cheese on top of chilies. Beat egg yolks. Add flour and milk. Beat egg whites and fold into egg yolk mixture. Add salt and pepper. Pour over cheese and press with fork into cheese. Bake at 325 degrees for 1/2 hour. Put thinly sliced tomatoes and remainder of chilies over top. Bake additional 1/2 hour.

## Rotgut Rodney's Refried Beans

Use canned or cooked **pinto beans**. Mash with potato masher, adding **1 teaspoon salt**. Usually 1/2 cup of hot **fat** is added when heating in a skillet, but you can heat in a sprayed non-stick skillet to keep item low fat. Shake **hot pepper sauce** on top.

## *Black Bart's Grilled Biscuits*

**1 can refrigerated biscuits**
**1 large onion, chopped**
**2 thinly sliced cloves garlic, optional**
**Butter**
**Seasoning salt**

Saute onion and garlic in butter until tender. Place biscuits in heavy foil. Cover with onion and garlic, pouring on the butter used when sauteing. Sprinkle seasoning salt on top. Bake according to package directions on grill or in oven.

## *Mr. Ed's Dill Biscuits*

**1 can refrigerated biscuits**
**1/4 cup melted butter**
**1 tablespoon dill weed**
**1 tablespoon onion soup mix**

Dip tops of biscuits in the melted butter, then in the dill weed that has been combined with the dry soup mix. Bake according to directions on package.

## Cow Punching Chili & Dumplings

1 pound ground beef
1 cup chopped onion
1 large can tomatoes
2 cans tomato sauce
1 tablespoon chili powder
2 teaspoons salt
1 can beans (optional)

Dumplings:
1 cup mashed potato flakes
1 cup flour
2 teaspoons baking powder
1/2 teaspoon salt
1 cup milk
1 egg
2 tablespoons oil

Make up chili and simmer until right before serving time. Combine flour, flakes, baking powder and salt. Mix milk with egg and oil and add to above. Stir to moisten. Let stand several minutes. Place spoonfuls on chili, cover tightly and cook 15 minutes.

## Country Corn Patch Bake

2 1/2 cups egg noodles
1 can whole kernel corn, drained
1 can cream of vegetable soup
3/4 cup milk
2 cups diced ham
1 cup grated cheddar cheese

Cook egg noodles until tender but still firm. Drain and place in deep casserole dish. Mix in all ingredients except cheese. Bake at 350 degrees for 30 minutes, adding cheese to top during the last five minutes in the oven.

## Wedding Dance Barbecue Sauce

1/4 cup olive oil
3/4 cup chopped onion
1 clove garlic, chopped
1 cup honey
1 cup catsup
1 cup vinegar
1/2 cup Worcestershire sauce
1 teaspoon dry mustard
1 1/2 teaspoons salt
1 teaspoon oregano
1 teaspoon black pepper
1/2 teaspoon thyme

Cook onion and garlic in olive oil until tender. Add remaining ingredients and simmer to blend flavors. The official Blum wedding barbecue sauce made by their Grandma Jean!

## Amber's Texas Style Marinade

4 servings steak
1/2 cup barbecue sauce (sweet or hot style)
1/4 cup catsup
2 tablespoons Worcestershire sauce
2 teaspoons hot pepper sauce
1 chili pepper, crushed
1 teaspoon lemon juice
1 teaspoon soy sauce
1 teaspoon seasoning salt

Mix all ingredients except steak in a plastic bag. Place steaks in bag and knead the marinade into steaks. Let stand for at least an hour on each side. The longer they are soaked, the spicier the steaks.

Hint: When grilling, brush remaining marinade on the steaks.

## Sunbonnet Sue's Meatloaf

Sue knew how to make a meatloaf that would be the talk of the county! Try it next time you have a backyard picnic.

**2 pounds lean ground beef**
**1 cup shredded carrots**
**1 jar spaghetti sauce**
**2 1/2 cups shredded potatoes**
**1 egg**
**1/2 cup mozzarella cheese**

Combine all ingredients except cheese and place in your favorite casserole dish. Bake 1 hour at 350 degrees, adding cheese during the last five minutes of baking.

## Pecos Pete's Potato Balls

Delicious with the meatloaf!

**1 large bowl filled with bread crumbs**
**1/2 medium onion, chopped**
**3 to 4 stalks celery, chopped**
**2 tablespoons parsley**
**1 1/2 cups milk, or enough to moisten**
**2 eggs, beaten**
**1 1/2 cups mashed potatoes**
**1/2 teaspoon salt**
**1/4 teaspoon pepper**
**1/2 pound butter, melted**

Add all ingredients except butter to bread crumbs. Mix well. Form into balls and place in buttered casserole. Pour melted butter over all and bake uncovered 20 minutes at 375 degrees.

## Juiciest Steak Ever, "Hereford Style"

**Steak**
**Oil or butter**

If grilling, broiling or pan frying steak, coat with thin layer of oil or butter. When you sear your steak this coating will hold in the juices rather than letting them boil or drip out of the meat. Sear steak with high heat, then cook to desired degree of doneness.

## Steak Sauce Western Style

1 bottle catsup
1/2 cup red wine
1/4 cup lemon juice
1/4 cup Worcestershire sauce
1 onion, chopped fine
3 garlic cloves, chopped fine
1 teaspoon chili powder
1/2 teaspoon salt
1/2 teaspoon dry mustard
1/2 teaspoon hot pepper sauce
1 teaspoon horseradish
1/2 cup brown sugar

Simmer until desired consistency. Refrigerate.

## Tornado Alley Sauerkraut

Large can sauerkraut, drained
Large can tomatoes
2 cups diced onions
1 pound bacon, chopped in small pieces

Brown bacon and onions. Add the tomatoes and the sauerkraut. Bake in 350 oven for 2 1/2 hours.

## "Chilly" Cowpoke Pie

1 pound ground beef
1 chopped onion
1 cup chopped celery
1/2 teaspoon salt
1 teaspoon chili powder
1 tablespoon Worcestershire sauce
8 ounces tomato sauce
1 package corn bread mix
1 cup shredded cheddar cheese

Brown the ground beef and drain off fat. Saute onion and celery. Combine and add remaining ingredients except corn bread mix and cheese. Place in casserole dish or pie pan. Make up the corn bread according to package directions and pour on top. Bake in 425 degree oven for 20 minutes. Top with cheese and return to oven to melt.

## Saddle Bag Eggs

6 hard boiled eggs
1 pound sausage
1 egg, beaten
1 cup bread crumbs

Wrap eggs completely with sausage. Dip in egg and then crumbs. Place on foil on grill. Cook 1/2 hour, turning regularly. Take off of foil and finish up by grilling an additional 15 minutes.

## Snuffy's Stuffed Grilled Onions

1 pound country sausage
2 cups stuffing mix or bread crumbs
Large onions, thickly sliced

Mix sausage and crumbs together and place between two slices of onion. Place each one in a square of foil that has been sprayed with a cooking spray. Grill for 1/2 hour.

## Chuckwagon Style Liver
Does your trail boss hate liver? Try this!

**2 pounds liver, sliced**
**1 large onion, sliced**
**1/2 pound sliced bacon**
**Salt and pepper**
**1 small can tomato sauce**

Layer onions and liver in baking dish. Add seasonings and bacon strips. Pour tomato sauce on top. Cover. Bake for 35 minutes in a moderate oven. Uncover and bake additional 10 minutes to brown.

## Western Lite Broil
**Top round, flank, or sirloin beef steaks**
**20 ounces soy sauce**
**10 ounces water**
**5 ounces lemon juice**
**5 ounces honey**
**1 2/3 tablespoons minced onion**
**1 1/4 teaspoons garlic powder**
**Sesame seeds, toasted**

Mix together all other ingredients then add steak. Marinate 24 to 48 hours. Broil beef to medium rare. Thin slice meat across grain. Sprinkle with toasted sesame seeds.

The recipe for Western Lite Broil is from the Cattlewomen's Association. As cattle producers, we want to thank them for the recipe and their promotion of beef.

## Cow Care Giver "Chicken Dinner"

Make up one of these for each cow care giver. Every once in a while they need some chicken!

**2 pieces chicken**
**1 small corn on the cob**
**Slices of:**

> **summer squash**
> **tomato**
> **onion**
> **potato**
> **green peppers**
> **carrots**

**Seasoning salt**
**Butter**

Place each "dinner" in several thicknesses of foil. Season and add a small amount of butter. Grill for 1 hour.

## *Gumbo's Grilled Sweet Potato*

Sweet potato or yam
2 tablespoons orange juice
1 tablespoon margarine
1/8 cup brown sugar

Peel sweet potato and cut into strips like shoe string potatoes. Place on a double thick piece of aluminum foil. Add the orange juice, margarine and sugar. Seal edges. Grill approximately 15 minutes, turning often.

## *Campfire Grilled Banana*

Banana
2 tablespoons brown sugar
Cinnamon or nutmeg

Leave banana peel on, just trimming ends. Slit one side of the peel and through the banana. Fill with the brown sugar plus sprinkle with cinnamon or nutmeg, if desired. Wrap in foil. Grill 15 minutes, turning frequently.

## *Poor Cowboy's Grilled Canned Ham*

Cook ham on foil until excess dripping quits. Then place directly on grill, but keep at least 8 inches from flame. Turn and brown, basting with marinade or sauce if desired.

## *Li'l Lyla's Ham Glaze*

1 cup brown sugar
1/2 teaspoon dry mustard
Wine vinegar

Mix together sugar, mustard and vinegar and use to baste or glaze ham. Use amount of vinegar needed to make consistency of your choice.

## Skillet Beef & Beans

1 pound of tender lean beef
2 tablespoons oil
1 chopped onion
2 cups French cut green beans, fresh or frozen
1 cup celery, sliced
1 tablespoon cornstarch
1 tablespoon soy sauce
1 can mushrooms
3/4 cup liquid (water and mushroom juice)

Cut beef into thin strips. Brown in oil. Add onion, beans and celery. Cook 4 to 6 minutes, stirring. Combine cornstarch with soy sauce and liquid. Add to skillet with mushrooms. Stir, cooking until liquid is shiny. Cover, cooking until beans are tender. Serve with rice.

## Mexican Dakota Casserole

1 pound hamburger
2 small cans tomato sauce
2 cans water
1/2 package chili flavoring mix
1/2 can refried beans
2 packages tortillas
1 1/2 to 2 cups shredded sharp cheddar cheese

Brown hamburger. Add sauce, water, chili flavoring and refried beans. Ladle 1/2 cup mixture into each tortilla. Place in layers in baking dish, pouring any remaining mixture over the top. Place cheese on top. Bake 15 to 20 minutes in 350 degree oven.

## Sad Sidney's Sombreros

1/2 cup chopped onions
1/2 cup chopped celery
1/2 teaspoon seasoning salt
1 tablespoon butter
1 pound hamburger
8 ounce can tomato sauce
1 can whole tomatoes
1 teaspoon taco sauce
1 teaspoon chili sauce
Corn chips
Lettuce
Cheese
Hot sauce
Sour cream

Saute onions and celery in butter, adding the seasoning salt while cooking. Brown the hamburger. Add the tomatoes, sauces, onions and celery. Simmer. Serve over corn chips, adding the lettuce, cheese, hot sauce and sour cream on top.

## Steer Wrestler's Steak Bake

This is a great recipe, but don't let the steer wrestler in your life provide the meat!

**1 1/2 pounds cube or sirloin steak**
**1/3 cup flour**
**1 teaspoon salt**
**1/4 teaspoon pepper**
**1 sliced onion**
**1/2 green pepper, sliced**
**1 pound can tomatoes**
**4 ounce can mushrooms, drained**
**3 tablespoons molasses**
**3 tablespoons soy sauce.**
**1 package frozen French cut green beans,**
    **thawed and drained**
**1 1/4 cups flour**
**1 1/2 teaspoons baking powder**
**1 teaspoon dry mustard**
**1/2 teaspoon salt**
**1/2 cup milk**
**2 tablespoons oil**
**1 egg**
**Sesame seeds**

Place meat in a 2 1/2 quart casserole dish. Sprinkle with the flour, salt and pepper; then toss. Bake uncovered at 400 degrees for 20 minutes. Add the onion, green pepper, tomatoes, mushrooms, molasses and soy sauce. Bake uncovered at 400 degrees for 30 minutes. Stir in the green beans. Make up muffins by combining the flour, baking powder, mustard and salt. Mix together the milk, oil and egg and add to dry ingredients all at once, stirring only until all dry particles are moist. Drop by tablespoons onto meat mixture and sprinkle with sesame seeds. Bake at 400 degrees for 15 to 18 minutes.

## Bootlegger's B B Q Beef

**Rump roast or brisket**
**1 can cola**
**1 bottle chili sauce**
**1 package dry onion soup mix**
**Salt and pepper**

Place in covered roasting pan and bake at 350 degrees until roast falls apart.

## Haluska

Nope, that's not your cowhand sneezing—just the name of this recipe from Brenda's mother!

**Large head of cabbage, chopped**
**1/2 pound bacon**
**1 chopped onion**

Dumplings:
**2 cups cooked grated potatoes**
**2 tablespoons flour**
**1 egg, beaten**
**1/2 teaspoon salt**
**1/8 teaspoon nutmeg**
**1/8 teaspoon pepper**

Fry bacon until crisp, crumble and set aside. Fry cabbage and onion in bacon grease, adding a little water to steam until tender. Mix together the potatoes, flour, egg, salt, nutmeg and pepper to make potato dumplings. Mix well and drop by spoonfuls over the cabbage mixture. Add bacon bits. Cover and steam for 8 to 10 minutes.

## Ranchhand Tamale Casserole

1 can tamales
1 can green chiles, diced
1 can cream style corn
1 cup grated cheddar cheese
1/2 cup minced onion
1/2 cup chopped green pepper
1/2 cup sliced ripe olives
1 teaspoon chili powder

Remove parchment from tamales and place in bottom of a flat casserole dish. Combine other items with the gravy from the tamales and pour on the top. Bake casserole at 325 degrees for 1/2 hour. Serve with sour cream.

## Bear Butte Spareribs

3 to 4 pounds ribs, cut into pieces
2 lemons, sliced thin
1 medium onion, sliced thin
2 cups tomato sauce
1/4 cup Worcestershire sauce
2 teaspoons chili powder
2 teaspoons salt
4 dashes hot pepper sauce
2 cups water

Place ribs, meaty side up in a pan with onion and lemon slices on top. Roast at 450 degrees for 30 minutes. Pour remaining ingredients over ribs and bake in medium oven 1 hour or until tender, basting often.

## Chucky's Chalupas for a Dozen

2 1/2 pound pork loin roast
2 1/2 pounds dry pinto beans
4 cloves garlic, chopped fine
2 tablespoons chili powder
2 teaspoons cumin
1 teaspoon oregano
1 tablespoon salt
2 Jalapeno peppers

Soak beans overnight. Place roast and beans in heavy Dutch oven pan. Cover with water. Add all seasonings, including garlic and peppers. Cover and cook 4 to 6 hours or until roast falls apart. Take out bones. Add water when cooking, if necessary.

Serve with:
Large package corn chips
4 chopped avocados
2 large onions, diced
2 heads lettuce, chopped
2 pounds cheddar cheese, grated
6 diced tomatoes
2 packages radishes, chopped
Chili sauce*

*Chili sauce:
1 medium onion, chopped
2 large tomatoes, chopped fine
1 tablespoon hot sauce
1 can green chilies
7 ounce bottle green taco sauce
Salt and pepper

Mix and let stand for 1 hour.

## Shady Sally's Deep Fried Tacos

1 1/2 pounds hamburger, browned and seasoned
2 teaspoons baking powder
2 1/2 cups flour
1 1/4 teaspoons salt
1 1/2 tablespoons shortening
1/2 cup warm water

Mix ingredients together except hamburger and knead a few minutes. Form into balls, rolling out into 5 inch circles. Place 1 tablespoon hamburger in shell. Fold and pinch shut. Deep fry in hot fat. Serve with usual taco "fixin's".

## Westward Ho Oriental Hamburger

1 pound hamburger
1 medium onion, chopped
1 cup chopped celery
1 can mushroom soup
1 can chicken soup
1 1/2 cans water
1/4 cup soy sauce
1/2 cup uncooked rice
1 can Chinese noodles

Brown hamburger and onion. Drain and add remaining ingredients except noodles. Place in baking dish. Bake, covered, at 350 degrees for 45 minutes. Remove cover, adding the Chinese noodles. Bake 15 to 20 additional minutes.

## Cowboy Style Coffee

Always start with cold water and a large coffee pot. Use approximately 1/2 pound coarse ground coffee for each gallon of water. Stir an egg and a small amount of water into the coffee grounds and place in a cheesecloth bag. Bring to a boil and simmer for 5 minutes. Remove from heat. If you have not used the cheesecloth bag, you will need to pour a cup of cold water on the top to settle the grounds. Enjoy.

## Corporal Sandy's Oven Fried Chicken

Doesn't this taste just like the chicken that guy in the army makes?

**3 cups self rising flour**
**1 teaspoon paprika**
**2 envelopes tomato soup mix**
**2 packages Italian dressing mix**
**1 teaspoon salt**
**Margarine, melted**

Mix up dry ingredients to use when making oven fried chicken. Take out only the amount needed and store the rest for future use. Dip pieces of chicken in margarine and coating. Place on cookie sheet so pieces do not touch. Brush on a heavy coat of melted margarine. Let set to dry surface. For extra crispy chicken, re-dip in the flour mixture, pressing into chicken and recoat with margarine. Bake at 350 degrees for one hour. For extra crispy chicken, baste every 15 minutes.

## Company's Coming Hot Dish

**4 cups cooked hamburger, reserve liquid**
**2 cups bread crumbs**
**2 cups cooked rice**
**4 eggs, beaten**
**3 cups liquid from hamburger,**
            **add water if necessary**
**1/4 cup chopped pimento**
**1 can cream of chicken soup**
**1 can cream of mushroom soup**
**1 chicken bouillon cube,**
            **dissolved in hamburger liquid**
**1/4 teaspoon pepper**

Combine all in a large baking pan and bake in moderate oven for an hour.

## Deputy Dan's Chili

1 pound hamburger
1 large can tomato sauce
1 heaping tablespoon onion flakes
1 can kidney beans
1 bean can of water (less dishes to wash!)
2 teaspoons chili powder
Salt and pepper

Brown hamburger and drain. Add remaining ingredients and bring to a boil. Reduce heat and simmer for 1 hour. "Eat it all up if you know what's good for you," says Deputy Dan.

~~~~~~~~~~~~~~~~~~~~~~~~~~~~~~~~~~~~~~~~~~~~~~

The above recipe Kay Andera, Chamberlain, SD, has included in her cookbook, *I Love Recipes*. It is from her son, Dan. Thanks, Kay, for letting us share this recipe in our book, too.

~~~~~~~~~~~~~~~~~~~~~~~~~~~~~~~~~~~~~~~~~~~~~~

## Ranch House Radish Pot Roast

3 to 4 pound chuck roast
Onions
Carrots
Potatoes
1 package radishes
1 package onion soup mix
Water

Brown roast in oil in a Dutch oven. Place roast on rack. Add small amount of water, cover and cook in oven or on top of stove at low temperature 1 1/2 to 2 hours. Add vegetables, more water and onion soup mix. Cover and cook until vegetables are tender. Thicken liquid to serve as gravy.

## Saloon Style Chicken Nuggets

3 tablespoons melted butter
2 teaspoons Worcestershire sauce
2 whole large chicken breasts
50 wheat wafers, finely crushed
1/3 cup grated Parmesan cheese

Place butter and Worcestershire sauce in bowl and stir. Cut skinned, boned chicken breasts into 1" pieces and toss in butter mixture to coat. Place wafers and cheese in a plastic bag. Add a few pieces of chicken at a time and shake to coat. Bake in a single layer at 450 degrees for approximately 8 to 10 minutes or until chicken is done and not pink.

Dipping Sauce:
1/4 cup brown sugar
1 tablespoon soy sauce
1 teaspoon cornstarch
1/2 cup white vinegar
2 tablespoons cold water
2 tablespoons minced fresh ginger

Mix sugar, soy sauce and vinegar together and heat until sugar dissolves. Mix cornstarch with water and add to sugar mixture. Stir until sauce boils. Remove from heat and add ginger.

## Porcupine Pete's Pepper Steak

1 1/2 pounds round steak
Seasoned flour
1 can onion soup
1/4 cup catsup
1 large green pepper cut in strips

Pound flour into meat. Brown steak in small amount of fat. Add soup and catsup and cook until tender, approximately 1 hour. Add green pepper and cook for an additional 20 minutes.

## Auctioneer's Ham It Up Loaf

2 pounds ground ham
1 pound sausage
2 eggs
1 cup bread crumbs
1 teaspoon dry mustard
1/2 teaspoon nutmeg
1 cup milk
Salt and pepper
1 cup brown sugar
1/4 cup water
1/4 cup catsup

Mix together all of the ingredients except last three. Place in loaf pan or casserole dish. Combine sugar, water and catsup and put on top. Bake in moderate oven approximately 45 minutes or until done.

## Zany Zach's Zucchini Bake

1 pound sausage
1 onion, chopped
1 can cream of chicken soup
1/2 cup bread crumbs
1 tablespoon dry parsley flakes
1 teaspoon salt
1/2 teaspoon sage
1/4 teaspoon pepper
4 ounces cheese spread
2 medium zucchini

Brown sausage with onion and drain off fat. Add remaining ingredients except zucchini. Split zucchini in half and top with the mixture. Bake 45 minutes to an hour in 350 degree oven.

## *Warren Clan Cowboy Beans*

**2 pounds hamburger**
**Dab of molasses**
**Handful of brown sugar**
**Large can of pork and beans**

Brown the hamburger. Duke says to add molasses and brown sugar until it looks good. Simmer. According to Marjean this turns out better when Duke makes it. Guess he knows what a dab and a handful are!

## *Roasted Mountain Oysters*
### (Warren Kids' Style)

At branding time, Marjean and Duke's four children love to help work the calves. Marjean never has to fix the kids a meal at the end of that day as they are full from roasting oysters over the branding fire. No details given! I can picture them roasting oysters on sticks over the fire like we cook hot dogs.

## Hot Ziggety Dog

2 tablespoons butter
2 8-ounce cans tomato sauce
1 clove garlic, minced
1 tablespoon sugar
1 teaspoon salt
1 teaspoon pepper
3/4 cup sour cream
2 pounds wieners
8 ounce package cream cheese
6 green onions, chopped
3/4 cup sharp shredded cheese
1 package egg noodles

Cut wieners into slices. Simmer with butter, tomato sauce, garlic, sugar, salt and pepper. Meanwhile, cook noodles according to package directions. Combine cream cheese and sour cream, beating until blended. Stir in onions. Arrange noodles in greased pan. Spoon cheese and onion mixture over noodles. Put tomato and wieners over that. Top with grated cheese. Bake at 350 degrees for 30 minutes.

## "Prairie" Chick'n Casserole

1 chicken, or pieces of your choice
2 cups water
1 1/2 cups rice
1 package dry onion soup mix
1 can chicken soup
1 can mushroom soup
1 cup milk

Mix together water, rice and onion soup mix. Place in 9x13 pan and place chicken on top. Heat remaining ingredients and pour over the chicken. Bake two hours at 350 degrees, uncovering last 30 minutes to brown.

## Trail Wagon Mock Pizza

1 1/2 cups cooked macaroni
2 eggs, beaten
2/3 cup milk
1 teaspoon salt
1/4 teaspoon pepper
1 teaspoon oregano
1/2 teaspoon basil
1 can tomato sauce
1/2 pound sausage, cooked and drained
1 cup shredded mozzarella cheese

Cook macaroni and drain. Add eggs, milk, salt and pepper. Pour into buttered pie pan and bake 25 minutes at 400 degrees. Mix oregano and basil with tomato sauce and pour over macaroni. Top with sausage and cheese and return to oven for 10 minutes.

## Duke's Cowboy Coffee

Simple--the way the Warren's made coffee! Put water in a kettle. Throw in some coffee. Boil. Drink it.

# Bronco Busting Bread

# WANTED

## *Breads and Quick Breads*

## Dancing Dixie's Fry Bread

2 cups self rising flour
1/2 cup nonfat dry milk powder
1 cup warm water

Combine above ingredients. Knead for a short while. Shape into balls that you can flatten into rounds. Fry in hot fat until golden brown on first side, turn and brown for a short amount of time on second side.

## Ice House Muffins

10 ounce box raisin bran cereal
1 cup melted shortening
3 cups sugar
4 eggs, beaten
1 quart buttermilk
5 cups flour
5 teaspoons baking soda
2 teaspoons salt

Will keep one month in refrigerator, but the cook is going to have to use it up fast if he's keeping it in his ice box in the chuckwagon. Fill muffin tins 2/3 full and bake at 400 degrees 15 to 20 minutes.

## Dakota Dorothy's Never Fail Dumplings

2 cups flour
1/2 teaspoon salt
4 level teaspoons baking powder
1 egg, slightly beaten
Milk

Place egg in cup and fill cup with milk. Add this to dry ingredients and beat a while. Let stand for 5 minutes. Drop by spoonfuls on broth and cook for 20 minutes tightly covered.

### Cowboy Size Pretzels

**Frozen bread dough, thawed**
**Egg white, beaten**
**Coarse salt**

Let dough rise to double. Divide into a dozen pieces and roll out into long ropes. Form into the pretzel shape. Gently boil in a skillet in which you have at least 2 inches of water. Cook until they rise, remove and drain. Brush with egg white or spray with water and sprinkle with salt. Bake on a greased cookie sheet for 20 minutes at 375 degrees.

### Black Skillet Corn Bread

**2 cups cornmeal**
**3/4 cup flour**
**1 1/2 teaspoons salt**
**1 teaspoon sugar**
**1 teaspoon baking powder**
**1/2 teaspoon baking soda**
**1/2 cup water**
**1 egg, beaten**
**2 cups buttermilk**

Combine dry ingredients. Add water beaten with egg and buttermilk. Heat oven to 450 degrees. While heating, place skillet in oven. Before pouring in batter, place several tablespoons shortening or bacon grease in skillet and heat. Pour batter into heated skillet and bake 20 to 25 minutes.

## Rough & Ready Refrigerator Rolls

**1 package yeast in 1/2 cup water**
**1/2 cup oil**
**1 teaspoon salt**
**1/2 cup sugar**
**1 cup milk**
**1 cup mashed potatoes**
**2 eggs, well beaten**
**5 cups flour, approximately**

Make up above ingredients into a stiff dough. Knead well. Place in oiled bowl and refrigerate overnight.

**For hamburger buns:**
Pinch off as needed. Let raise to 2 to 3 times dough size. Bake 20 minutes at 350 degrees.

**For sweet rolls:**
Melt the following in double boiler and drizzle over rolls before letting raise.
**6 ounce package butterscotch chips**
**1/4 cup light corn syrup**
**2 tablespoons water**
**2 tablespoons butter**

## Deadwood Drop Doughnuts

**3 cups flour**
**1 cup sugar**
**2 teaspoons baking powder**
**1/2 teaspoon salt**
**1/2 teaspoon nutmeg**
**2 eggs**
**1 cup milk**

Mix together dry ingredients. Beat eggs, adding milk. Mix into dry ingredients. Drop into hot fat and fry 3 to 5 minutes.

## Bull Rider's Bean Bread

**1 cup raisins (use 1/2 golden raisins)**
**1 cup water**
**1 cup oil**
**3 eggs**
**1 cup white sugar**
**1 cup brown sugar**
**1 pound can pork and beans**
**3 cups flour**
**1 1/2 teaspoons cinnamon**
**1/2 teaspoon baking soda**
**1 teaspoon vanilla**
**1 cup walnuts, chopped**

Place raisins in water and bring to a boil. Remove and let set to absorb water. Beat pork and beans until not chunky. Beat oil and sugar; then beat in 3 eggs, one at a time. Add pork and beans. Add dry ingredients, then stir in vanilla, raisins and nuts. Bake in two loaf pans at 350 degrees for one hour.

## Diane's Li'l Buckaroo Blueberry Bread

6 tablespoons softened margarine
1 cup sugar
2 eggs
1 1/2 cups flour
1 teaspoon baking powder
1/4 teaspoon salt
16 ounce can blueberries, drained and rinsed
1/2 cup milk
2 teaspoons lemon rind
1/3 cup sugar
3 tablespoons lemon juice

Cream butter with electric mixer. Add sugar, beating at medium speed until well blended. Add eggs one at a time, beating after each. Combine flour, baking powder and salt. Gently dry the blueberries. Remove 1/2 cup of the dry mix and dust the berries. Add the balance of flour mix alternately with the milk, beginning and ending with the flour mixture. Stir in lemon rind. Gently, gently fold in blueberries. Pour into prepared 8x4x3 loaf pan. Bake at 350 degrees for 55 to 60 minutes or until toothpick in center comes out clean. Combine the 1/3 cup sugar with lemon juice in small pan and heat until sugar dissolves. Puncture top of bread in several places with toothpick. Pour mixture over warm bread, allowing it to soak into the bread. Cool in pan 30 minutes before removing.

## Bunk House Butter Biscuits

**2 cups flour**
**1 tablespoon baking powder**
**1 teaspoon salt**
**1 tablespoon sugar**
**6 tablespoons butter**
**2/3 cup milk**
**1 egg**

Combine flour, baking powder, salt and sugar. Cut in butter until dough is the size of peas. Combine milk and egg and mix into flour mixture with a fork. Pat out to 1/2 inch thickness and cut. Bake on an ungreased cookie sheet in a 425 degree oven for 8 to 10 minutes.

## Lazy J Coconut Coffeecake

**3 cups flour**
**1/3 cup sugar**
**4 1/2 teaspoons baking powder**
**1 1/2 teaspoons salt**
**1 1/4 cups oatmeal, uncooked**
**3/4 cup shortening**
**3 eggs, beaten**
**1/2 cup milk**
**3/4 cup melted butter**
**3/4 cup honey**
**1/3 cup shredded coconut**

Mix dry ingredients together. Add oatmeal. Cut in the shortening. Mix eggs and milk together and stir into dry ingredients only until all is dampened. Drop by heaping tablespoons into ungreased 9x13 pan. Combine melted butter and honey. Pour over dough and sprinkle with the coconut. Bake at 400 degrees 20 to 25 minutes. Honey and butter will sink to bottom while coconut stays on top. Serve warm, but you'll need a fork--delicious but messy!

## Cornmeal Griddle Cakes for a Crowd

3 cups flour
2 teaspoons baking powder
1 teaspoon salt
2 cups cornmeal
6 eggs, slightly beaten
4 cups milk
3/4 cup shortening, melted

Mix flour, baking powder, salt and cornmeal. Combine eggs, milk and shortening. Add to dry ingredients and beat until smooth. Bake on lightly greased griddle until bubbles break and edges are cooked before turning.

## A "maize"ing Pancakes

1 egg
1 1/2 tablespoons shortening
1 1/2 cups flour
1 1/2 teaspoons sugar
1 teaspoon baking powder
1/2 teaspoon salt
1 1/2 cups buttermilk
1/2 cup whole kernel corn

Beat egg. Add shortening and dry ingredients. Gradually beat in buttermilk. Stir in the corn. Bake on heated, greased griddle until bubbles appear. Turn and finish cooking.

## Slim Jim's Pancakes

1 1/2 cups flour
1 3/4 teaspoons baking powder
1 teaspoon salt
4 tablespoons butter, melted
4 tablespoons brown sugar
1 1/4 cups milk
2 eggs, separated

Combine dry ingredients. Add brown sugar that has been mixed with the melted butter plus milk and egg yolks. Whip egg whites until stiff and gently fold into the batter. This should make approximately 8 to 10 large pancakes.

~~~~~~~~~~~~~~~~~~~~~~~~~~~~~~~~~~~~~~~~~~~~

My Dad wrote this about Gilbert Crazy Bull:

In the early 1920's Lower Brule would have a "fair", and the Indian people would come from miles around and camp at the edge of the fair grounds. They would celebrate by having rodeo's, dancing and baseball games.

Gilbert Crazy Bull was a handsome Indian cowboy and one of the very best cowboys that ever straddled a horse. He used to ride at this event. He and Walt Schrieber would even ride out double on a bronc. Gilbert was little known as he never got to the "big time" rodeos.

~~~~~~~~~~~~~~~~~~~~~~~~~~~~~~~~~~~~~~~~~~~~

## Dizzy Lizzy's Zucchini Bread

**1 1/2 cups flour**
**1 teaspoon cinnamon**
**1/2 teaspoon baking soda**
**1/4 teaspoon baking powder**
**1/4 teaspoon salt**
**1/4 teaspoon nutmeg**
**1 cup sugar**
**1 cup unpeeled zucchini, finely shredded**
**1/4 cup applesauce**
**2 egg whites**

Combine flour, cinnamon, baking soda, baking powder and nutmeg. In separate bowl, mix together sugar, zucchini, applesauce and egg whites. Add the flour mixture, stirring only until combined. Pour batter into greased loaf pan. Bake in 350 degree oven for 55 to 60 minutes or until a toothpick inserted near center comes out clean. Cool for 10 minutes on wire rack before removing. This freezes well. You can substitute apple for the zucchini for a different flavor.

## Red Rock Biscuits

These biscuits aren't hard as rocks like you might think from the name!

**2 1/2 cups baking mix**
**2 tablespoons sugar**
**3/4 teaspoon cinnamon**
**1/2 cup raisins**
**1/2 cup chopped nuts**
**2/3 cup milk**

Mix together well. Knead for a minute or two. Roll or pat out and cut. Bake approximately 10 minutes. You may want to frost while warm with a powdered sugar glaze.

## Ranch Land Fruit Bread

**1/2 cup butter**
**1 cup sugar**
**1 beaten egg**
**1 1/2 cups applesauce**
**1 teaspoon vanilla**
**2 teaspoons baking soda**
**1/2 teaspoon cinnamon**
**2 cups flour**
**1 cup chopped dates**
**1 cup walnuts, chopped**
**1 cup raisins**
**1/2 cup maraschino cherries, drained**
**1/2 cup crushed pineapple**

Cream butter and sugar well.  Add beaten egg, then applesauce
and vanilla.  Combine dry ingredients and add to the mixture.
Add dates, nuts, raisins, cherries and pineapple.  Pour in bread
pan lined with waxed paper.  Bake at 350 degrees for 1 hour and
15 minutes.

## Kirby's Pluckets

1 package yeast
1/4 cup lukewarm water
1 cup scalded milk
1/3 cup sugar
1/3 cup butter
1/2 teaspoon salt
3 eggs, beaten
3 1/2 to 4 cups flour
Melted butter
3/4 cup sugar
1/2 cup ground nuts
3 teaspoons cinnamon

Dissolve yeast in water. Add sugar, butter and salt to the milk and cool to lukewarm before adding yeast mixture. Add the eggs and enough flour to make a soft dough. Cover and let rise. Make dough up into small balls. Dip in butter and roll in the sugar, nut and cinnamon mixture. Pile loosely in a tube pan. Let rise again before baking. Bake 10 minutes at 400 degrees and 30 more minutes at 350 degrees until nicely browned. Invert pan immediately over serving dish. Let everyone "pluck" their own rolls.

## Mary Liz's Moonlighting Coffee Cake

Yellow cake mix
1 package vanilla instant pudding mix
4 eggs, 8 egg whites or 1 cup egg beaters
1 cup plain nonfat yogurt
1/4 cup applesauce
1 can whole cranberry sauce

Blend all except cranberries together. Beat on high for 3 minutes, scraping bowl often. Spread 3/4 of batter in prepared 9x13 pan. Spoon cranberry sauce evenly over it. Pour remaining batter on and spread. Bake 55 to 60 minutes at 350 degrees. Cool for 35 minutes.

## Rustler's Raisin Bread

2 cups milk, scalded
2 cups cold water
2 packages yeast
3/4 cup sugar
3 teaspoons salt
6 tablespoons margarine
2 eggs
11 to 12 cups flour
1 1/2 cups raisins

Cool milk with water. Add yeast and sugar, letting dissolve. Add salt, margarine, eggs and enough flour to make a paste. Beat well. Add the rest of flour and beat again. Add raisins. Knead and let rise. Knead and put in pans. Let rise. Bake 40 to 45 minutes at 375 degrees.

## Lineshack Whole Wheat Bread

3 cups milk, scalded
1 cup lard or shortening
1 cup honey
3 teaspoons salt
3 cups water
6 cups whole wheat flour
3 packages yeast,
          dissolved in 1/2 cup warm water
White flour

Add milk to next three ingredients, stirring until dissolved. Add cold water to cool to about 120 degrees. Add flour and yeast and beat with mixer until smooth. Add enough white flour until stiff enough to knead. Grease bowl and knead for 10 minutes. Let rise in bowl, punch down and make up into 5 loaves. When raised, bake at 350 degrees about 30 minutes.

## Dina's Rebel Rousing Rolls

**Frozen cinnamon rolls**
**1 container frozen whipped topping, thawed**
**1 cup brown sugar**
**1/2 stick margarine, melted**
**Pecans**

Mix together whipped topping, sugar and margarine. Place in bottom of baking pan. Sprinkle with pecans. Place cinnamon rolls on top and let rise. Bake carefully in medium oven until golden brown. Let cool slightly before inverting to remove from pan.

ITS SPECULATED THE CONTINUOUS UP & DOWN MOTION OF BUTTER CHURNING RESULTED IN EITHER...

CASES OF CARPAL TUNNEL SYNDROME

..OR...

FORMIDABLE ARM WRESTLERS

## Matt Dillon's Rhubarb Muffins

3/4 cup brown sugar
1/2 cup oil
1 egg
1/2 cup yogurt or buttermilk
1 teaspoon vanilla
1 cup flour
1 cup oatmeal
1/2 teaspoon baking soda
1 cup finely sliced rhubarb
1/4 cup brown sugar
1/2 teaspoon cinnamon

Mix together the sugar, oil, egg, yogurt and vanilla. Stir in the dry ingredients just until mixed. Add rhubarb. Put in greased muffin tins and sprinkle with the sugar and cinnamon. Bake at 350 degrees for 20 minutes.

# CATTLE DRIVE COOKIES AND CANDIES

# WANTED

Cookies and Candies

## Esther's Small Town Macaroons

6 egg whites
1/2 teaspoon cream of tartar
1 2/3 cups sugar
1 teaspoon vanilla
1 teaspoon vinegar
1/4 teaspoon baking powder
2 cups crushed corn flakes
1 cup coconut

Beat egg whites and cream of tartar until stiff. Add sugar 2 tablespoons at a time and beat. Stir in vanilla, vinegar, and baking powder. Add corn flakes and coconut. Drop on cookie sheet and bake at 325 degrees for 10 to 12 minutes. Let cool on wax paper.

## Rocky Point Rolled Molasses Cookies

1 cup sugar
1 cup lard
2 eggs
1/2 cup dark molasses
3 cups flour
2 teaspoons ginger
1 teaspoon cinnamon
1 teaspoon nutmeg
1/2 teaspoon allspice
2 tablespoons boiling water
    mixed with 1 tablespoon baking soda

Cream sugar and lard. Beat in eggs. Add remaining items and beat. Add more flour if needed. Roll out very thin. Cut with cookie cutter. Sprinkle with sugar. Bake in 350 oven for approximately 10 minutes.

## *Annie Oakley's Apple Bars*

Crust:
**1 1/4 cups shortening**
**3 cups plus 2 tablespoons flour**
**1/4 teaspoon salt**
**1 egg yolk**
**1 slight cup milk**

Topping:
**7 to 8 cups sliced apples**
**1 3/4 cups sugar**
**3 tablespoons flour**
**1/2 teaspoon cinnamon**
**2 tablespoons margarine**
**1 egg white**

Mix crust together like pie crust, adding the egg yolk that has been beaten with a fork into the milk. Roll dough into two crusts several inches longer than a jelly roll pan. Place a crust on the jelly roll pan. Spread with apples. Sprinkle with sugar, flour and cinnamon. Dot with margarine. Place top crust over apple mixture. Beat the egg white with fork until it will spread easily over the crust. Bake at 375 degrees about 40 to 45 minutes. Frost with a powdered sugar icing.

## *Barn Dance Popcorn Balls*

**1 small package fruit flavored gelatin**
**1 cup sugar**
**1 cup white syrup**
**1 teaspoon baking soda**

Mix together and heat to boiling. Take off burner and add soda. Mixture will expand. Pour over approximately 4 quarts popped corn and shape into balls.

## LeAnn's Favorite Farmer's Chip Cookies

1 1/2 cups white sugar
1 1/2 cups brown sugar
1 cup shortening
1 cup margarine
2 teaspoons vanilla
3 eggs
2 3/4 cups flour
1 1/2 teaspoons baking soda
1/2 teaspoon baking powder
3 cups oatmeal
2 cups chocolate chips (or raisins)

Mix the first six ingredients in a large bowl. Add flour, soda and baking powder. Stir in oatmeal and chips, mixing well. Bake at 350 degrees for 12 minutes, preferably on air bake pans.

## "Dr. Jay Penniworth's" Cheese Curls

Have you heard the expression "to die for"? These caramel cheese curls are it!

Large package cheese curls
2 cups brown sugar
1 cup margarine
1/2 cup dark corn syrup
1/2 teaspoon baking soda

Cook sugar, margarine and corn syrup, boiling for 5 minutes. Remove from heat and stir in soda. Pour this mixture over cheese curls in a large baking pan. Bake in 250 degree oven for 1 hour, stirring to separate after 10 minutes.

### Poker Face Pat's Almond Roca

1 cup real butter
1 cup sugar
2 tablespoons corn syrup
3 tablespoons water
1/2 cup slivered almonds
1/2 package chocolate chips

Melt butter in saucepan. Add sugar, corn syrup and water. Boil
until hard crack. Brown almonds on a cookie sheet. Pour mixture over the almonds and spread. Pour chocolate chips on top.
They will melt, and you can spread them over the almond mixture. Let harden and break up.

### Lolli's Lollipops

18 lollipop sticks
1/4 cup margarine
1/2 cup light corn syrup
3/4 cup sugar
Flavoring, if desired
A few drops food coloring

Lightly butter baking sheet. Arrange sticks on sheet. Combine
butter, syrup and sugar in heavy quart pan. Heat to boiling, stirring occasionally. Reduce heat and stir and cook to 270 degrees.
Stir in food coloring and flavoring. Drop mixture by tablespoons
over each stick.

## Rocky Ridge Raisin Squares

1 cup raisins
1/2 cup water
1 cup sugar
2 eggs
1 teaspoon baking soda
1/2 teaspoon salt
1 teaspoon cinnamon
1/2 teaspoon nutmeg
2 cups flour
1 cup sour cream

Cook raisins in water until dry. Beat eggs with sugar. Add dry ingredients alternately with sour cream. Stir in raisins. Spread as thin as possible on greased, floured cookie sheets. Bake at 350 degrees until lightly browned. Glaze with powdered sugar frosting and cut while still warm.

## Grandma For's Ice Box Cookies

Make these ahead and have them in the freezer. Just pull a roll out when unexpected company drops in, and in a few minutes you will have cookies to go with coffee.

1 cup butter
2 cups brown sugar
1 teaspoon vanilla
2 eggs
3 1/2 cups flour
1 teaspoon baking soda
Dash of salt
1 cup nut pieces

Cream butter and sugar. Add vanilla and eggs, beating well. Mix in remaining ingredients. Make into rolls and freeze or refrigerate until ready to slice and bake. Bake at 350 degrees for 10 minutes.

## Best In The West Sugar Cookies

These are the "melt in your mouth" kind of cookies. Pack them in empty coffee cans if taking them out to have with "campfire coffee"; you don't want any broken cookies.

1 cup powdered sugar
1 cup white sugar
1 cup butter
1 cup oil
2 eggs
1 teaspoon vanilla
4 cups plus 4 heaping tablespoons flour
1 teaspoon salt
2 teaspoons baking soda
1 teaspoon cream of tartar

Cream powdered sugar, white sugar, butter and oil. Beat in eggs and vanilla. Sift and add remaining ingredients. Place walnut size balls of dough on non-stick cookie sheet and flatten with fork. Bake 8 to 10 minutes at 375 degrees.

FIRST STAGE
FOR
**BUTTER
COOKIE
RECIPE**
(OPTIONAL)

## Agnes's Saddle Up Sugar Cookies

1 cup vegetable shortening
1 cup butter flavored vegetable shortening
1 cup powdered sugar
1 cup granulated sugar
2 eggs
4 cups flour
1 teaspoon cream of tartar
1 teaspoon baking soda
Flavoring to taste

Cream shortening, adding sugars and eggs. Add dry ingredients. Add flavoring such as 1 to 1 1/2 teaspoons vanilla. Chill well. Roll in small balls and flatten on cookie sheet with glass dipped in sugar. Bake 8 to 10 minutes in 350 degree oven.

## The Chicken Farmer's One Cookie

This is great fun for kids.  Sorry about the mess in the kitchen!

**1 tablespoon beaten egg**
**1/4 teaspoon vanilla**
**2 teaspoons brown sugar**
**Dash of cinnamon**
**2 tablespoons rolled oats**
**Pinch of salt**
**1 tablespoon flour**
**1/2 tablespoon applesauce**

Mix well.  Bake at 350 degrees for 10 minutes.

## Sandhills Shortbread

**1 cup real butter**
**1/2 cup powdered sugar**
**1 cup flour**
**1/2 cup corn starch**

Mix other ingredients into butter.  Make into balls, and flatten with fork.  Bake at 325 degrees for 20 minutes.

## School Daze Skillet Brownies

**4 squares unsweetened chocolate**
**1 1/2 sticks butter or margarine**
**3 large eggs**
**1 1/2 cups sugar**
**1 teaspoon vanilla**
**1 cup flour**
**1 cup walnuts, chopped**

In heavy saucepan melt chocolate and butter.  Beat eggs.  Add sugar, vanilla and eggs to chocolate mixture.  Set heat on low.  Add flour. Stir in nuts.  Grease a 10 inch skillet.  Pour mixture into skillet.  Cook over low heat for 30 minutes.  Mixture will start pulling away from sides when done.  Cool.  May be inverted to remove from skillet, or cut into wedges in skillet.  Sprinkle with powdered sugar.

## Tavern Tillies's Toffee Bars

1 cup margarine
1 cup brown sugar
1 egg yolk
1 teaspoon vanilla
2 cups flour
1/4 teaspoon salt
1 large package chocolate chips
2 tablespoons margarine

Combine all ingredients except chips and last margarine. Put in 10x13 pan and bake at 350 degrees for 20 to 25 minutes. Melt chips with margarine and spread over bars while warm.

## Wagon Wheel Cookies

Make up the following twice, once using a chocolate mix and then a yellow mix. Pat out light colored layer of dough over dark and roll up. Chill, slice and bake to make cookies that look like wagon wheels.

**1/3 cup oil**
**2 eggs**
**1 cake mix**

Mix together as explained above and bake in moderate oven on greased cookie sheet until starting to brown.

## Windy Acres Waffle Iron Cookies

**4 egg yolks**
**2 sticks margarine**
**1 1/2 cups sugar**
**2 cups flour**
**1/2 teaspoon salt**
**1 teaspoon vanilla**
**4 egg whites, beaten until stiff**

Cream egg yolks with margarine and sugar. Add flour, salt and vanilla. Fold in egg whites. Drop from teaspoon on waffle iron set on low heat. Cook approximately 1 minute. Note: no baking soda or baking powder.

## Badlands Bon Bons

**1 cup butter**
**1/3 cup powdered sugar**
**3/4 cup cornstarch**
**1 cup flour**
**Chopped nuts**

Blend butter and powdered sugar well. Add cornstarch and flour and mix. Chill dough. Make into balls, dipping tops in nuts. Place on ungreased cookie sheet and flatten with glass. Bake 15 minutes at 350 degrees. When cool frost with a powdered sugar frosting.

## Buffalo Chip Bars

2 2/3 cups flour
2 1/2 teaspoons baking powder
1/2 teaspoon salt
2/3 cup shortening
2 1/2 cups light brown sugar
3 eggs
1 cup chopped nuts
1 package semi-sweet chocolate chips

Mix together dry ingredients. Melt shortening. Stir in brown sugar and let cool slightly. Beat in the eggs, one at a time. Stir in flour mixture plus nuts and chips. Pour into greased 15x10x1 pan. Bake 25 minutes at 350 degree oven.

## Uncle Wiggles's Carrot Bars

2 cups flour
2 cups sugar
4 eggs
1 1/4 cups cooking oil
3 teaspoons cinnamon
3/4 teaspoon salt
2 teaspoons baking soda
2 cups grated carrots

Mix together all ingredients. Pour into greased jelly roll pan and bake 30 minutes at 375 degrees. When cool, frost with cream cheese frosting:

3 ounces cream cheese
1 stick margarine
2 teaspoons vanilla
2 or more cups powdered sugar

Beat frosting well before spreading.

## *Prairie Rose's Peanut Brittle*

**1 stick margarine**
**2 teaspoons baking soda**
**1 cup water**
**1/2 teaspoon salt**
**1 cup white syrup**
**2 heaping cups sugar**
**2 cups raw Spanish peanuts**

Melt margarine and mix with soda.  Set aside.  Cook water, salt and syrup to crack stage.  Add peanuts and cook approximately 10 minutes or until peanuts are golden brown.  Continue stirring, turning off heat, and add margarine mixture.  Pour onto buttered cookie sheet.

## "Road Apple" Cookies

1 cup finely chopped apples
1/4 cup raisins
1/4 cup chopped pecans
1/2 cup sugar
2 tablespoons water
1 cup margarine
1 cup brown sugar
2 eggs
2 cups flour
2 teaspoons baking powder
1 teaspoon cinnamon
1/2 teaspoon salt
1/2 teaspoon cloves
1/2 cup milk
2 cups quick cooking oatmeal

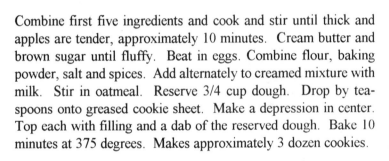

Combine first five ingredients and cook and stir until thick and apples are tender, approximately 10 minutes. Cream butter and brown sugar until fluffy. Beat in eggs. Combine flour, baking powder, salt and spices. Add alternately to creamed mixture with milk. Stir in oatmeal. Reserve 3/4 cup dough. Drop by teaspoons onto greased cookie sheet. Make a depression in center. Top each with filling and a dab of the reserved dough. Bake 10 minutes at 375 degrees. Makes approximately 3 dozen cookies.

## Grandpa Jones's Peanut Butter Popcorn

2 to 3 quarts popped popcorn
1/2 cup sugar
1/2 cup corn syrup
1/2 cup peanut butter
1 teaspoon vanilla

Place popcorn in an ice cream bucket. Bring sugar and corn syrup to a boil. Add peanut butter and vanilla. Pour over popcorn.

## Wild 'N Wooly Walnut Squares

These are super rich so cut them small. But be prepared to make a second batch right away.

1 cup brown sugar
1 egg
1 teaspoon vanilla
1/2 cup flour
1/4 teaspoon baking soda
1/4 teaspoon salt
1 cup walnut pieces

Stir together sugar, egg and vanilla. Do not beat. Sift flour, soda and salt and add to above mixture. Then stir in walnuts. Place in greased 8" pan. Bake 20 minutes at 350 degrees. Cut into small squares.

## Round Up Cookies

These are sometimes called Cowboy Cookies, but cowgirls like them, too!

1/2 cup shortening
1/2 cup brown sugar
1/2 cup sugar
1 egg, beaten
1 tablespoon water
1 teaspoon vanilla
3/4 cup flour
1/2 teaspoon baking soda
1/2 teaspoon salt
1 1/2 cups oatmeal
1 1/4 cups chocolate chips
1 cup walnuts, chopped
Optional: 1 cup raisins

Cream shortening and sugars. Add egg, water and vanilla, then dry ingredients. Beat well. Add chips and nuts. Bake 10 to 12 minutes at 375 degrees until cookies are starting to brown, but still are soft.

## Truck Stop Lemon Bars

These are so tangy and delicious. Note the unusual crust.

**6 tablespoons butter**
**3/4 cup brown sugar**
**1 cup flour**
**1/2 teaspoon baking soda**
**1/2 teaspoon salt**
**1/3 cup flaked coconut**
**1/2 cup finely crushed saltines**
**3/4 cup granulated sugar**
**2 tablespoons cornstarch**
**1/4 teaspoon salt**
**1 cup hot water**
**2 beaten egg yolks**
**1/2 teaspoon grated lemon peel**
**1/2 cup lemon juice**

Cream butter and brown sugar; stir in next 5 ingredients. Press 1/2 mixture into 8" pan. Bake 350 degrees for 10 minutes. In saucepan combine sugar, cornstarch and salt. Gradually stir in water. Cook and stir until thick and bubbly. Boil 2 minutes. Remove from heat. Stir small amount hot mixture into egg yolks; return to pan. Cook and stir until boiling. Remove from heat. Gradually stir in lemon peel and juice. Pour over crust; top with reserved crumbs. Bake at 350 degrees for 30 minutes or until lightly browned.

## Mrs. McGillacutty's Great Grahams

24 graham cracker squares
1/2 cup melted butter
1/2 cup brown sugar
1 cup chopped nuts

Line jelly roll pan with foil. Place crackers on foil. Mix butter with brown sugar and spoon over the crackers. Sprinkle with nuts. Bake in moderate oven at 350 degrees for 10 to 12 minutes. Cut into squares while warm. Remove to cooling rack.

## Slack Time Soda Cracker Toffee

1 cup brown sugar
1 cup butter (no margarine)
12 ounces chocolate chips
40 to 42 soda crackers

Line jelly roll pan with foil. Place crackers in a layer on foil. Boil butter and brown sugar 3 minutes (no more) and pour over crackers. Bake at 400 degrees for just 5 minutes. Remove from oven, put chocolate chips on top and spread as they melt. Cut these while warm.

## Who Needs Sugar Cookies

1/2 cup raisins
1/2 cup dates
1/2 cup prunes
1 cup water
1/2 cup margarine
1 egg
Pinch of salt
1 teaspoon vanilla
1 cup flour
1 teaspoon baking soda
1 teaspoon cinnamon

Boil fruit in the water for 3 minutes. Add margarine and cool. Add remaining ingredients and mix well. Refrigerate for several hours. Drop onto greased cookie sheet. Bake at 350 degrees until light brown.

## Who Needs Flour Cookies

This is the recipe you may have heard of as monster cookies. It makes a big batch (11 dozen) of cookies even though it doesn't have any flour in it.

10 eggs
2 cups brown sugar
2 cups white sugar
1 1/2 teaspoons vanilla
1 1/2 teaspoons white corn syrup
4 teaspoons baking soda
1 cup margarine
3 cups chunky peanut butter
9 cups oatmeal
1 pound (hard covered) chocolate candy drops

Mix in ingredients in order given. When well blended, drop onto cookie sheet. Bake at 350 degrees for 10 minutes.

### Ornery Ole's Orange Applesauce Brownies

1 cup brown sugar
6 tablespoons margarine
1/2 cup applesauce
1 beaten egg
1 teaspoon orange peel
1 teaspoon vanilla
1 1/4 cups flour
1 teaspoon baking powder
1/2 teaspoon salt
1/4 teaspoon baking soda
1/2 cup chopped walnuts

In saucepan combine brown sugar and margarine. Cook and stir over medium heat until margarine melts. Remove from heat and beat in applesauce, egg, orange peel and vanilla. Stir in flour, baking powder, salt and soda. Add nuts. Spread in greased jelly roll pan. Bake at 350 degrees about 15 minutes. While warm, top with a powdered sugar glaze to which you have added 2 tablespoons orange juice.

### Suicide Creek Coconut Bars

1/2 cup margarine
1/2 cup brown sugar
1 cup flour
1 cup sugar
2 eggs
1 teaspoon vanilla
2 tablespoons flour
1/2 teaspoon baking powder
1 teaspoon salt
1 cup coconut
1/2 cup nuts

Mix together margarine, brown sugar and cup of flour. Pack into greased baking pan. Bake at 360 degrees for 10 minutes. Cream sugar, eggs and vanilla. Add remaining ingredients and pour and spread over crust. Bake 20 more minutes.

## Cowpoke Cheesecake Bars

12 ounce package butterscotch chips
1/3 cup margarine
2 cups graham cracker crumbs
1 1/4 cups chopped nuts
8 ounce package cream cheese, beaten until fluffy
14 ounce can sweetened condensed milk
1 egg
1 1/2 teaspoons vanilla

Melt margarine and chips in saucepan. Stir in crumbs and nuts
and press 1/2 of this into bottom of large cake pan. Beat together
remaining ingredients and pour over crust. Top with remaining
crumbs. Bake at 350 degrees for 20 to 30 minutes or until toothpick comes out clean.

## Champion Chocolate Cookies

For the chocolate lover who likes a softer cookie.

1 1/4 cups margarine
2 cups sugar
2 eggs
2 teaspoons vanilla
2 cups flour
3/4 cup cocoa
1 teaspoon baking soda
1/2 teaspoon salt
1 cup chopped nuts

Cream margarine and sugar. Add eggs and vanilla. Stir in flour,
cocoa, soda and salt. Then add nuts. Drop onto ungreased baking sheet. Bake at 350 degrees for 8 to 9 minutes.

## Big Bend Oatmeal Cookies

3 eggs, well beaten
1 cup raisins
1 teaspoon vanilla
1 cup shortening or margarine
2 cups sugar, 1 white, 1 brown
2 1/2 cups sifted flour
2 teaspoons baking soda
3/4 teaspoon salt
1 1/2 teaspoons cinnamon
2 cups oatmeal
1 cup chopped nuts

Combine eggs, raisins and vanilla. Thoroughly cream together
the shortening and sugars. Add dry ingredients and mix well.
Blend in eggs, raisins, oatmeal and nuts. Dough will be very stiff.
Roll dough into small balls, flatten and put on ungreased cookie
sheet. Bake at 350 degrees until starting to brown.

## Burnt Sugar Candy

3 cups white sugar
Small amount of water
1 cup light cream
1/2 teaspoon vanilla
1/8 teaspoon baking soda
1/4 cup butter
1 cup nuts, chopped

Melt 1 cup of the sugar in heavy skillet over low heat, stirring
constantly until melted. Add a small amount of water and cook
until caramel colored. Pour the rest of the sugar and the cream
slowly into the burned sugar mixture. Cook slowly to firm ball
stage, stirring constantly. Remove from fire and add soda. Stir
vigorously. Add butter and cool 10 minutes. Add vanilla and
beat until mixture loses its shine and is thick. Add nuts and pour
into buttered pan.

## Saddle Bum Bar Cookies

**White cake mix**
**2/3 cup butter**
**1/4 cup brown sugar**
**3 eggs, separated**
**1 tablespoon white sugar**
**1 cup chocolate chips**
**1/3 cup almonds**

Combine cake mix, brown sugar, butter and egg yolks. Pat into jelly roll pan. Beat egg whites with sugar until stiff. Spread over dough. Sprinkle on the chips and almonds. Bake 20 to 25 minutes at 350 degrees.

## Velma's "Can't Get A Date" Bar

**1/2 cup butter**
**1 cup brown sugar**
**1 1/2 cups flour**
**1/2 teaspoon salt**
**1 teaspoon baking soda**
**1 3/4 cups quick cooking oatmeal**
**1 pound dates, pitted and chopped**
**1 cup sugar**
**1 cup water**

Cream butter and sugar; add dry ingredients and mix until crumbly. Firmly pat 1/2 the mixture in greased 9x13 inch pan or pan lined with waxed paper. Make up date filling by slowly cooking dates with sugar and water until consistency of jam. Be sure to watch so this doesn't burn. Spread over crust in pan. Add remaining crumbs and pat smooth. Bake in 350 oven for 25 to 30 minutes. Cut into bars or squares. Serve as is or with whipped cream.

# COWBOY CAKES

# WANTED

*Cakes and Frostings*

*For those who just like to eat the frosting:*

## Mud Hollow Frosting

1/2 cup margarine, melted
6 tablespoons milk
2 1/2 tablespoons cocoa
1 cup miniature marshmallows
1 pound box powdered sugar
1 1/2 teaspoons vanilla

Melt margarine. Add milk, marshmallows and cocoa, stirring until melted. Remove from heat. Add sugar and vanilla and beat well. Spread while still warm.

## Cactus Flats Fudgy Frosting

6 tablespoons milk
1/2 cup butter
4 tablespoons cocoa
Powdered sugar
1 teaspoon vanilla

Mix together the milk, butter and cocoa. Heat and boil for two minutes. Add powdered sugar to make the right consistency to beat. Beat. Add vanilla.

## Lulu Belle's Buttermilk Icing

1 cup sugar
1/2 cup buttermilk
1/4 teaspoon baking soda
1 teaspoon vanilla
1/2 cup butter

Cook first three ingredients until soft ball. Add butter and vanilla and beat until it starts to thicken. Quickly pour on the cake and spread.

## Frank's Banana Frosting

1 ripe banana
2 cups powdered sugar
1/2 teaspoon almond or vanilla extract
Chopped walnuts or almonds, if desired

Thoroughly blend banana, powdered sugar and extract. Stir in nuts.

## Burnt Sugar Cake

1 cup sugar
1 cup boiling water
1 1/2 cups sugar
1/2 cup butter
3 egg yolks
1 cup milk
2 1/4 cups flour
3 teaspoons baking powder
1/2 teaspoon salt
3 egg whites, stiffly beaten

Put first sugar in heavy skillet and cook slowly to a golden brown, stirring constantly. Add boiling water and dissolve over low heat. Reserve 4 tablespoons for icing.

Cream second sugar and butter. Add egg yolks, beating well. Add 2 tablespoons burnt sugar mixture alternately with milk. Add dry ingredients and beat for 3 minutes. Fold in the egg whites. Bake in 3 8-inch cake pans that have been greased and floured. Bake 25 minutes in 350 degree oven. When cool, frost with the following:

Frosting:
2 cups sugar
4 tablespoons burnt sugar syrup
1 cup cream

Cook together until soft ball stage. Beat until creamy.

## Bucking Bronc Blueberry Cake

Top with a dollop of sweetened sour cream mixed with fresh blueberries! Wow!

2/3 cup sugar
1/4 cup butter or margarine
1 egg
1 cup flour
1/2 teaspoon salt
1/2 teaspoon baking soda
1 teaspoon cream of tartar
1/2 cup milk
2 cups blueberries
1/4 cup flour, for dredging
1 cup sour cream
3 tablespoons powdered sugar

Cream sugar and butter. Beat in egg. Add dry ingredients alternately with milk. Stir 1 cup of the blueberries mixed with dredging flour into mixture. Put in greased pan and bake at 375 degrees for 30-35 minutes. Mix balance of blueberries with sour cream and powdered sugar to use as the topping.

## Razzle Dazzle Red Velvet Cake

2 1/2 cups flour
2 cups sugar
6 tablespoons cocoa
2 tablespoons baking soda
4 eggs, well beaten
2 cups sour cream
1 teaspoon vanilla

Combine eggs, sour cream and vanilla. Stir in dry ingredients and beat for 3 minutes at low to medium speed. Bake in greased and floured pan for 45 minutes at 350 degrees. Frost when cool.

## Long Trail Home Cupcakes

2 cups flour
2 cups sugar
2 sticks margarine
3 tablespoons cocoa
1 cup water
1/2 cup buttermilk
2 eggs
1 teaspoon baking soda
1 teaspoon vanilla

Place margarine, cocoa and water in saucepan. Bring to a boil. Add the sugar and stir. Cool. Add flour and stir. Mix balance of items together and add to first mixture. Bake in cupcake papers for 15 to 20 minutes at 375 degrees.

## Ladies' Poker Party Cake

1 cake mix
4 eggs
2/3 cup oil
1 package strawberry gelatin
1 package strawberries, thawed

Mix all ingredients together and bake in prepared cake pan at 325 for 50 minutes.

## Mud Flap Cake

**2 cups sugar**
**4 eggs**
**1 cup milk**
**2 cups flour**
**1 teaspoon baking powder**
**1 teaspoon vanilla**
**1 small jar peanut butter**
**1/2 pound chocolate bar**

Cream sugar and eggs. Add milk, dry ingredients and vanilla and mix well. Bake in greased jelly roll pan at 350 degrees until sides are crusty and pull away. Let cool 3 minutes. Spread with peanut butter. Refrigerate for 10 minutes. Melt candy bar and spread over peanut butter. Cut before chocolate hardens. Store in refrigerator.

## Pumpkin Patch Cake

2 cups sugar
1 cup oil
4 eggs
2 cups pumpkin
2 cups flour
1/2 teaspoon salt
1 teaspoon cinnamon
1 1/2 teaspoons baking soda
2 teaspoons baking powder

Cream sugar and oil. Add eggs and pumpkin. Mix in dry ingredients and beat well. Bake in greased and floured 9x13 pan 35 to 40 minutes at 350 degrees. Serve with cider sauce or frost with cream cheese frosting.

Frosting:
Blend **8 ounce package cream cheese**, **1 stick margarine** and **1 teaspoon vanilla.** Add **powdered sugar** until thick but still of a spreadable consistency.

## Cider Sauce

2 cups cider
1 tablespoon lemon juice
1 teaspoon grated lemon peel
1 cup sugar
2 tablespoons cornstarch
1/2 teaspoon cinnamon, optional
2 tablespoons butter

Cook together all but butter; adding butter after mixture has thickened and you have removed pan from heat. Serve over cake.

## *Daylight Chocolate Date Cake*

1 cup chopped dates
1 1/2 teaspoons soda
1 1/2 cups boiling water
3/4 cup margarine
1 cup sugar
2 eggs
1 3/4 cups flour
3/4 teaspoon baking soda
1/8 teaspoon salt
3/4 cup sugar
6 ounces chocolate chips
1 cup chopped walnuts

Soak dates in boiling water and soda until cool. Cream margarine, first sugar and eggs and add to date mixture. Beat in flour, soda and salt until well blended. Pour into greased and floured 9x13 pan. Cover with the last sugar, chocolate chips and nuts. Bake 45 minutes at 350 degrees.

## *"Spurred On" Cake*

1 cup oatmeal
1 1/2 cups boiling water
1/2 cup shortening
1 1/2 cups sugar
2 eggs
1 cup flour
1/2 cup cocoa
1 teaspoon baking soda
1/2 teaspoon salt
1 teaspoon vanilla

Mix oatmeal with boiling water. Let cool. Cream shortening, sugar and eggs. Add oatmeal mixture and remaining ingredients. Beat until smooth. Bake in greased and floured 9x13 pan at 350 degrees for 35 minutes.

## Out Back Oatmeal Cake

1 cup quick cooking oatmeal
1 1/2 cups boiling water
1 stick margarine
1 cup white sugar
1 cup brown sugar
1 1/2 cups flour
1 teaspoon baking soda
2 eggs
1 teaspoon cinnamon
1/4 teaspoon salt
1 teaspoon vanilla

Mix oatmeal with water and let cool. Cream sugar and margarine. Add eggs then dry ingredients and vanilla. Bake in 11x 7 inch pan for 30 to 40 minutes at 350 degrees. Top with the following and broil until starting to brown:

1 cup brown sugar
1 cup coconut
1/2 cup evaporated milk
4 tablespoons margarine
1/2 cup nuts

## Horse Crazy Cake

1 package lemon cake mix
1 box instant vanilla pudding
4 eggs
1/2 cup oil
1 cup liquid (skim milk or use 1/2 milk, 1/2 water)
3/4 cup poppy seeds

Mix all ingredients together and beat for five minutes. Grease bundt cake pan well. Sprinkle with **cinnamon** and **sugar**. Bake 45 minutes at 350 degrees. Let set to cool for 15 minutes before taking out of pan.

## Mary Liz's Rich Chocolate Cake

1 cup applesauce
1/2 cup cocoa
2 cups sugar
4 egg whites
1/2 teaspoon salt
2 1/4 cups all purpose flour
1 cup buttermilk
1 teaspoon vanilla
2 teaspoons baking soda
1 cup hot water

Combine applesauce, cocoa and sugar in mixing bowl and beat on low speed until well mixed. Add eggs; beat on medium speed. Add salt, buttermilk, flour and vanilla on low speed, then beat on high for 2 minutes. Add soda to hot water. Gradually mix into cake batter. Batter will be thin. Pour into layer pans (2) or a 13x9x2 pan that has been greased and floured. Bake at 375 degrees for 40 minutes.

## Berry Surprised Cake

White cake mix, prepared
2 cups miniature marshmallows
2 packages frozen strawberries, thawed
2 packages strawberry gelatin

Place marshmallows in bottom of 9x13 pan. Pour prepared cake mix over top. Mix the strawberries and gelatin together and pour over cake batter. Bake 50 to 60 minutes at 350 degrees. Let cool and serve with whipped cream.

## Geneva's Volcano Cake

Chocolate cake mix, prepared
1 cup nuts
1 cup coconut
8 ounce package cream cheese
1 stick margarine
3 1/2 cups powdered sugar

Place nuts and coconut in a greased 9x13 pan. Pour on the cake mix made up according to directions. Place cream cheese and margarine in microwave and soften. Blend together. Add powdered sugar and drizzle over cake mix. Bake at 350 degrees 30 to 40 minutes or until done.

## Draft Horse Upside Down Cake

1 cup flour
2 teaspoons baking powder
1/2 teaspoon salt
3/4 cup sugar
2 tablespoons shortening
1/2 cup milk
1 teaspoon vanilla
1 cup nuts
1/2 cup sugar
1/2 cup light brown sugar
1/4 cup cocoa
1 cup boiling water

Combine dry ingredients with first sugar. Soften shortening and add with milk and vanilla. Stir in nuts. Mix well. Pour into greased baking dish. Combine last sugars and cocoa. Sprinkle on batter. Pour boiling water over all. Do not stir. Bake 45 minutes at 350 degrees. Cool and serve topped with whipped cream or ice cream.

# DALLY UP DESSERTS

# WANTED

*Delicious Desserts*

## Ruff N Ready Pie

1 cup milk
Large package of marshmallows
1 package of frozen whipped topping, thawed
1 package miniature chocolate chips
2 cups graham cracker crumbs
1/8 to 1/4 cup margarine, melted

Melt marshmallows in the milk, then cool. Mix in the whipped topping, then the chocolate chips. Before putting in a pie pan, line the pan with graham cracker crumbs mixed with melted butter, reserving 1/4 cup of crumbs to sprinkle on top. You can double the recipe and use a 9x13 pan.

## Bedroll Blueberry Grape Dessert

2 packages grape gelatin
20 ounces blueberry pie filling
15 ounces crushed pineapple (drained)

Prepare gelatin with 2 cups hot water. Add pie filling and pineapple. Pour into 13x9 pan. Chill until firm.

Topping:
8 ounces cream cheese, softened
12 ounce container sour cream
1/2 cup sugar
1/4 teaspoon vanilla
1 cup walnuts, chopped

Mix topping ingredients except nuts until creamy. Spread on top of gelatin mixture. Sprinkle with nuts.

## Margie's Stampede Pie

1/3 cup sugar
3 tablespoons cornstarch
1/4 teaspoon salt
1 1/2 cups milk
2 egg yolks
2 tablespoons butter
1 teaspoon vanilla
1/2 teaspoon almond extract
3 tablespoons sugar
3 to 4 bananas, sliced
2 egg whites
1 single 10" pie crust, baked (smaller, use less bananas)

Combine sugar. cornstarch and salt. Blend in milk and egg yolks and cook until thick and bubbly. Remove from heat. Stir in butter, vanilla and almond. Cool to room temperature. Beat egg whites to soft peaks, gradually adding the 3 tablespoons sugar. Fold into the cream mixture. Alternate layers of cream mixture and bananas in crust. Cover and chill. Top with frozen whipped topping.

## Dr. Time's Oreo Dessert

24 oreo cookies
1/8 cup melted margarine
Vanilla ice cream
Fudge ice cream sauce, the thick "spooning" kind
Frozen whipped topping, thawed
Chopped nuts

Make up dessert in four layers. Crush cookies in a plastic bag. Add margarine and mix. Pat into a 9x13 inch pan. Slice the ice cream and place slices over cookie crust. Spread with the fudge sauce, then a layer of whipped topping. Sprinkle with nuts. Freeze.

## Penelope's Snowy River Pavlova

Pennie moved to Australia. We miss her, but we get to enjoy some unusual recipes shared by her.

**6 egg whites**
**1 1/2 cups caster sugar (white)**
**2 teaspoons corn flour (cornstarch)**
**1 teaspoon vinegar**
**1 teaspoon vanilla**
**1 1/2 cups cream, whipped**
**Fruit**

Beat egg whites until stiff peaks form. Gradually add sugar, beating well until egg whites are thick and glossy. Fold in corn flour, vinegar and vanilla. Spread mixture in a circle on a pizza type pan (line to be sure no grease is on pan). Bake in preheated 260 degree oven on low rack for 35 to 45 minutes. Turn oven off and leave in oven until cool. Spread whipped cream on top and place slices of fresh fruit on cream. Use strawberries, banana, maraschino cherries, pineapple, etc.

## Wyatt Earp's Apple Pie & Cheddar

Pastry for 2 crust pie
7 cups sliced apples (tart)
2/3 cup sugar
4 teaspoons flour
1 1/2 teaspoons cinnamon
Cheddar cheese slices

Mix together sugar, flour and cinnamon. Place half of the apples in pie crust. Sprinkle with half of the sugar mixture. Fill pie crust with balance of apples and top with the rest of the sugar. Cover with top crust, sealing at edges and cutting slits for steam to escape. Bake at 450 degrees for 10 minutes, then approximately 50 minutes at 350 degrees. Serve warm topped with a slice of cheddar cheese.

## Hitchin' Post Dessert

2 small packages lemon flavored gelatin
3 cups boiling water
1 package miniature marshmallows
8 ounce package cream cheese
1 cup salad dressing
1 cup maraschino cherries, drained
1 cup crushed pineapple, drained
1/2 cup chopped walnuts, optional
1 cup heavy cream, whipped

Dissolve gelatin in boiling water  Add marshmallows, salad dressing and cream cheese. Stir until softened and well blended. Cool until partially set. Add cherries, pineapple, whipped cream and nuts. Refrigerate. This takes longer time to set than most gelatin desserts.

## Lazy Cowpoke No Bake Peach Pie

1 cup water
1/4 cup sugar
2 tablespoons corn starch
1 small package peach gelatin.
4 very ripe peaches, peeled and sliced thin
1 cooked pie shell

Cook water, sugar and corn starch until it comes to a boil. Let cool, then stir in the gelatin. Toss peaches in the gelatin mixture and pour into pie shell. Chill. Serve with whipped cream or ice cream.

## Wranglin' Apple Bread Pudding

4 slices bread, broken in chunks
1 1/2 cups applesauce
1/8 teaspoon cinnamon
Dash of nutmeg
2 tablespoons butter
2 cups milk
2 beaten eggs
1/2 cup sugar
1/2 teaspoon vanilla
Dash of salt
Cinnamon

Place 1/2 of the bread in a buttered 8x8 pan. Combine applesauce with cinnamon and nutmeg and spread over bread. Place remainder of bread on top and dot with the butter. Combine remaining ingredients and pour over bread mixture. Lightly sprinkle with cinnamon. Bake uncovered at 350 degrees for 1 hour.

## "Spotted Ass" Strawberry Dessert

1/2 cup oil
2 tablespoons milk
1 1/2 cups flour
2 tablespoons sugar
1/2 teaspoon salt

Stir oil and milk together. Pour into flour, sugar and salt. Blend
with pastry fork and pat into 9x13 pan, covering bottom and 3/4
inch up sides. Bake at 375 degrees for 12 to 15 minutes.

Filling:
Fresh strawberries
2 cups water
2 cups sugar
4 tablespoons cornstarch
1 small box strawberry flavored gelatin
Whipped cream

Cool crust. Then fill with fresh strawberries. Cook water, sugar
and cornstarch until thick. Remove from heat and stir in dry
gelatin. Pour over berries. Chill. Serve with whipped cream.

## Trading Post Peach Cobbler

2 quarts fresh peaches
1 1/4 cups sugar
2 tablespoons corn starch
1/2 teaspoon salt
2 tablespoons lemon juice
1/2 teaspoon almond extract
3 tablespoons margarine
2 cups baking mix
1 cup grated sharp cheese
4 tablespoons melted margarine
2/3 cup milk

Place peaches in greased 9x13 baking dish. Mix sugar, corn starch and salt; sprinkle over peaches. Sprinkle on lemon juice and almond extract and dot with margarine. Bake at 400 degrees for 15 minutes. Meanwhile, mix baking mix with cheese. Add margarine and milk. Drop dough on hot peaches. Return to oven and bake 20 minutes.

## Bubba's Dutch Babies

Very popular in the Dutch heritage areas of Iowa.

2 tablespoons butter
1/2 cup flour
1/2 teaspoon salt
1/2 cup milk
2 eggs, beaten
2 tablespoons butter, melted
Fruit and whipped topping

Heat first butter in pie pan in 425 degree oven. Beat all ingredients except butter until smooth. Add melted butter. Pour into heated pan. Reduce heat and cook at 350 degrees for approximately 20 minutes. Prick the puffy shell and return to oven for another 5 to 10 minutes. Fill shell with your choice of fruits. Cut as pie and serve with whipped topping.

## Edith's Auction Day Pudding

If you've ever sat at your bull sale on a bad day, you'll know why Mom and I would rather be home baking!

1 cup pitted dates, chopped
1 cup boiling water
1/2 cup white sugar and 1/2 cup brown sugar
1 egg
2 tablespoons butter, melted
1 1/2 cups flour
1 teaspoon baking soda
1/2 teaspoon baking powder
1/2 teaspoon salt
1 cup chopped nuts
1 1/2 cups brown sugar
1 1/2 cups boiling water
1 tablespoon butter

Combine dates and boiling water. Set aside. Stir together white sugar, brown sugar, egg and butter. Add dry ingredients. Stir in nuts and the date mixture. Pour into 11x7 inch baking dish. Pour on sauce made with brown sugar, water and butter. Bake at 375 degrees for 40 minutes. Cut in squares, invert and serve with whipped cream.

## "Stable" ized Whipped Cream

1 cup heavy cream
1/4 cup powdered sugar
1 teaspoon vanilla
1/2 teaspoon gelatin
1 tablespoon cold water

Soften gelatin in cold water for 5 minutes. Place over simmering water until dissolved. Allow to cool but not gel. Whip cream until barely stiff (holds good peaks). Beat in gelatin all at once, just long enough to incorporate. Add sugar and vanilla. Store in covered container in refrigerator.

## O'Grady's Green Apple Slice Delight

2 1/2 cups flour
1 tablespoon sugar
1 teaspoon salt
1 cup shortening
1 egg, separated
Milk
2/3 cup crushed corn flakes
5 cups peeled and sliced apples
1 1/2 cups sugar
1 teaspoon cinnamon
1 cup powdered sugar
2 tablespoons lemon juice

Mix together flour, sugar and salt and cut in shortening. Put egg yolk in cup and add enough milk to make 2/3 cup. Add flour mixture and mix just enough to make a ball. Pat 1/2 out on baking sheet. Cover with corn flakes, then apples. Sprinkle on sugar and cinnamon. Roll out balance of dough and place on top, pinching edges. Beat egg whites until stiff and spread on top crust. Bake at 400 degrees for 40 minutes. While hot, drizzle with glaze made of the powdered sugar and lemon juice.

## Cattle Kate's Cheesecake

**3/4 cup flour**
**1 teaspoon baking powder**
**1/2 teaspoon salt**
**1 egg**
**3 1/4 ounce package regular vanilla pudding mix**
**3 tablespoons margarine**
**1/2 cup milk**
**15 ounce can sliced peaches**
**8 ounces cream cheese**
**1/2 cup sugar**
**3 tablespoons juice from peaches**
**1 tablespoon sugar**
**1/2 teaspoon cinnamon**

Combine flour, baking powder, salt, egg, pudding, margarine and milk. Beat 2 minutes and spread in pan. Drain peaches and arrange over top of batter. Beat cream cheese with the 1/2 cup sugar and the juice for 2 minutes. Spoon over batter to within 1 inch of edge of pan. Sprinkle sugar and cinnamon over top. Bake at 350 degrees for 30 to 35 minutes or until crust is golden brown.

..I GOT THE RECIPE FROM THAT NICE MAN THATS WRITING FOR A PARDON...

# Wild West Recipes

# WANTED
### Wild Game Recipes

## Cody's Pheasant Cordon Bleu

1/2 cup melted butter
1 teaspoon lemon and pepper seasoning
1 teaspoon paprika
4 boned pheasant breasts, pounded with tenderizer mallet
4 thin slices ham
1 cup stuffing mix, prepared
Cheese slices, optional
Water or bouillon

Combine butter and seasonings and brush over pheasant breasts. Place a slice of ham, cheese (if you like ) and 1/4 cup stuffing mix on the breasts. Roll up and fasten with toothpicks. Brush outsides of rolls with balance of seasoned butter. Bake in covered roaster on a rack in 350 degree oven for 1/2 hour, adding small amount of water or beef bouillon. Remove cover and bake additional 30 minutes. Serve with Brown Butter Sauce.

Brown Butter Sauce:
2 tablespoons butter
1 to 2 tablespoons flour
2 cups beef bouillon

Brown butter until golden. Stir in flour. Add beef bouillon Cook, stirring, until thickened.

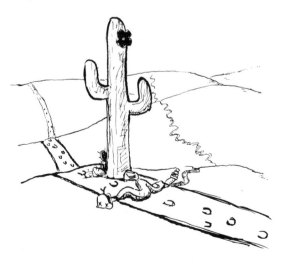

## Travis & Scott's Pheasant Feast

**Pheasant or other game bird**
**Seasoned bread crumbs**
**Egg**
**Water**
**Bacon**

Pound pheasant breast until thin. Grind the balance of the meat and mix with bread crumbs and egg. Add enough water so stuffing will stay in a ball. Form the size of a baseball. Wrap pheasant breast around this; then wrap with bacon. Fasten with toothpicks. Bake in moderate oven until done, at least 1 hour.

## Back In The Saddle Beer Batter Fish
### You'll like fish this way!

**1 can beer**
**1 teaspoon salt**
**1/2 teaspoon pepper**
**Flour**
**Fish fillets**

Combine beer, salt, pepper and enough flour to make a thin batter. Dip fish in batter and fry in hot fat.

## Western Pheasant Parmesan

**Pheasant pieces, deboned and pounded**
**Parmesan cheese**
**Flour**
**Salt**
**Pepper**
**Mayonnaise**

Spread pheasant with mayonnaise. Dip in equal parts of cheese and seasoned flour. Brown carefully in small amount of fat until crispy golden brown.

## Skeeter's Walleye & Salsa Soup

2 cups water
1 cup instant rice
Walleye fillets, 1 to 1 1/2 pounds
4 cups chicken bouillon
1 jar chunky salsa
1 package frozen mixed vegetables
1 lemon, sliced very thin
Sour cream

Simmer rice and mixed vegetables in water for 5 minutes. Add chicken bouillon and bring to a boil. Chop fish into small pieces and cook until flaky. Add salsa and bring to a simmer. Serve in bowls with lemon slice and sour cream on top.

## Saddle Blanket Salmon & Snow Peas

1/4 pound snow peas
1 pound fettuccine
1 pound fresh salmon fillets
3/4 teaspoon salt
1/2 teaspoon pepper
2 tablespoons butter
1 cup heavy cream
1 tablespoon lime juice
1 teaspoon chopped dried dill

Cook fettuccine until tender. Cook snow peas only until crisp tender. Season salmon with salt and pepper. Fry salmon in the butter until lightly browned. Place on a plate and set aside. Add cream and lime juice to skillet. Boil until reduced in half. Add snow peas and reheat. Remove from heat and stir in dill and any remaining salt and pepper. Place pasta in a large serving bowl. Shred salmon and place in bowl. Add cream and snow peas and toss.

## *Last Round Up Pheasant*

**2 to 4 pheasants, cut up**
**1 cup diced celery**
**1/4 cup chopped onions**
**1/2 pound sliced mushrooms**
**1/2 cup dry white wine**
**2 cups chicken broth**
**1 pint sour cream**
**Butter**
**Flour**

Dredge pheasants in flour. Brown in butter. Remove to heavy roaster. Saute vegetables until onions are clear. Pour over pheasants. Add 4 more tablespoons flour and butter to frying pan. Add chicken broth and wine, cooking until thick and smooth. Remove from heat. Stir in sour cream and pour over pheasants. Bake at 350 degrees for 1 1/2 to 2 hours.

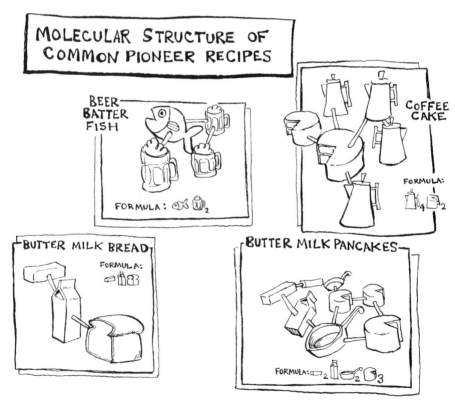

MOLECULAR STRUCTURE OF COMMON PIONEER RECIPES

BEER BATTER FISH

FORMULA:

COFFEE CAKE

FORMULA:

BUTTER MILK BREAD

FORMULA:

BUTTER MILK PANCAKES

FORMULA:

## Quick Draw Pickled Fish

Cut fish such as northern pike into bite size pieces.

1. Soak in strong salt water (will float an egg) for 48 hours.

2. Drain, rinse and cover with white vinegar for 24 hours.

3. Drain and wash with spray. Should be white and crisp.

4. Make brine by boiling together the following:

    **1 1/2 cups white vinegar**
    **2 bay leaves**
    **3 whole cloves**
    **2 1/2 teaspoons pickling spice**
    **2 cups sugar**
    **1 teaspoon whole peppercorns**
    **1/2 teaspoon whole allspice**

When brine has cooled, add 1 cup white table wine. Layer fish with sliced onions. Pour brine over all. May be eaten in several days.

## Jim Just Cooked His Goose

**Goose fillets**
**Apples, sliced**
**Onions, sliced**
**Garlic powder**
**Salt**
**Pepper**

Place a layer of sliced apples and onions in bottom of roaster. Lay goose fillets on top and season with garlic, salt and pepper. Add more apples and onions on top. Cover and bake at 325 degrees until done.

## Wild John's Horse Bite Steak

**Venison steaks or**
      **breast of grouse**
**Mustard horseradish**
**Flour**
**Salt**
**Pepper**

Pound meat out well into thin steaks.  Spread both sides with mustard horseradish.  Dip in flour.  Lightly salt and pepper.  Fry in a hot skillet until nicely browned and crisp.

# WANTED

*Time and Labor Savin' Recipes*

A PIONEER SPORTING RALLY...

## Fast Fletcher's Lasso Lasagna

**1 pound ground beef or turkey**
**1 package taco seasoning mix**
**8 ounces shredded cheddar cheese**
**4 6-inch corn tortillas**
**1 can red kidney beans, undrained**
**1/2 cup picante sauce**

Brown meat and drain.  Add seasoning mix and blend.  Reserve 1/4 cup of the cheese.  Place 1 tortilla in bottom of 2 quart casserole dish.  Top with 1/4 of the meat and 1/4 of the remaining cheese.  Repeat layers three times.  Pour beans including liquid over top.  Cover with picante sauce and sprinkle with reserved cheese.  Microwave uncovered on high for 6 to 8 minutes until hot.  This will make 6 servings unless you eat fast; then it only serves three.

..WHATS THE 'HALF-LIFE' OF THIS CHILI?

## Stable Kids' Forgotten Chicken Dinner

2 cups rice, raw
1 can cream of celery soup
1 can cream of mushroom soup
1 cup water
1 chicken, cut up
1 package dry onion soup mix

Butter or grease 9x13 baking pan. Put in rice. Heat soups and water and pour over rice, stirring gently. Place chicken pieces on top and sprinkle on the onion soup mix. Cover with foil and bake 2 1/2 hours in medium oven.

## Professor Plumtree's Cocoa
Makes one cup, only!

1 teaspoon cocoa
1 tablespoon sugar
2 tablespoons very hot water
1 cup milk
1/4 teaspoon vanilla
Marshmallows or whipped cream

Combine cocoa and sugar in small saucepan. Stir in water until well dissolved. Add milk. Heat to near boiling. Stir in vanilla. May be made in microwave.

## Log Cabin Olive's Casserole

2 pounds beef stew meat, chopped and tenderized
2 medium onions, chopped
1 can tomato soup
1 small jar olives with liquid

Put all in 2 quart casserole dish and bake at 350 degrees for 3 hours. Serve on rice or chow mein noodles.

## Lone Wolf Casserole

**3 ounces dried beef, chopped**
**1 can mushroom soup**
**1 cup milk**
**1 cup uncooked macaroni**
**1 cup grated cheese**
**1 small onion, diced**

Mix together and place in casserole dish.  Cover and let set overnight or all day before baking 30 to 35 minutes in 350 degree oven.

## Rawhide Patties

1 cup walnuts, chopped fine
2 cups cottage cheese, small curd
1 onion, chopped
5 eggs, beaten
1 cup bread crumbs, dry
1 teaspoon salt
1 teaspoon poultry seasoning or sage

Mix together and form into patties.  Brown in small amount of hot fat.

## Dusty Road Beef Ribs

3 pounds beef ribs
1 thick sliced onion
1 can cola
1 cup catsup
2 tablespoons Worcestershire sauce
1 tablespoon chili powder
2 teaspoons garlic salt
1 teaspoon onion powder
1 teaspoon black pepper

Combine all ingredients in crock pot and cook all day.

## Turn Out Chicken Bake

A gourmet style microwave recipe.

**6 chicken breasts, without skin**
**4 tablespoons butter**
**1 teaspoon salt**
**1 teaspoon pepper**
**1 can french fried onion rings**
**1 cup grated Swiss cheese**
**1 cup sliced mushrooms**

Melt butter and add salt and pepper. Roll chicken in butter. Arrange in baking dish. Cover with waxed paper and cook on high for 5 minutes. Turn chicken over, cover with mushrooms and cook on high for 4 minutes. Sprinkle top with onion rings then add cheese over all. Cook on high for 3 more minutes.

# OXEN vs MULES

| CHARACTERISTICS: | | |
|---|---|---|
| **HORSE POWER** | NONE (WRONG SPECIES) | 1/2 INHERIT TO EACH |
| **FUEL CAPACITY** | RUMINATE BOVINE POWER | 1 STOMACH |
| **WARRANTEE** | LIMITED TO THE LIFE OF EACH OX | LIMITED TO LIFE OF EACH MULE |
| **DEALER INCENTIVES** | FERTILIZER SUPPLY, ONE-TIME MEAL DESIGN, FLY BAIT | PROVIDES A WALKING, HE-HAWING ABNORMAL PSYCHOLOGY COURSE |
| **STRUTS** | ONLY AROUND ATTRACTIVE FEMALE OF SAME SPECIES | ONLY AT WILL |
| **RESALE** | USUALLY A MARKET AT LEAST FOR PARTS | VARIABLE |

## Recipes For Those Who Love Barbecued Chicken:

### Mule Creek B.B.Q Chicken

1 chicken
1 cola
1 cup catsup

Cook in covered roaster in oven or can be cooked in crock pot.

### Big Country B.B.Q Chicken

1 chicken, cut up
1 cup tomato puree
1/4 cup catsup
1 tablespoon oil

Place chicken in baking dish, skin side down. Cover with 1/2 of sauce made from remaining ingredients. Cover and bake 30 minutes. Uncover and put on the rest of sauce, baking for another 30 minutes to 1 hour or until tender.

### Buck Board Chicken

1 chicken, cut up
1 bottle catsup
2 teaspoons dill pickle relish
1 teaspoon Italian seasoning
Juice of one lemon
1 tablespoon dried onions
1/2 box brown sugar

Mix barbecue ingredients and pour over chicken. Bake at 400 degrees for approximately 1 hour.

# Pork Ala Honky Jonk

1 1/2 tablespoons oil
1 1/2 tablespoons salt
4 pork chops, thick cut
1 tablespoon oil
1 teaspoon salt
1 tomato, peeled and diced
1 celery heart, sliced
1 cup chopped lettuce
1/4 cup sliced onion
1/2 cup water
2 teaspoons cornstarch in 3 tablespoons water
1/4 cup catsup
2 tablespoons Worcestershire sauce
2 teaspoons sugar
1/8 teaspoon pepper

Heat first oil and salt in fry pan. Saute pork chops for 30 to 40 minutes. Remove bones and cut into 1/2 inch squares. Add the tomato, celery, lettuce and onion with the next tablespoon of oil and the teaspoon of salt and saute 1 minute, stirring constantly. Add water. Cover and cook 1 minute. Add meat. Cook 1 minute more, covered. Stir in cornstarch paste and remaining ingredients. Cook, stirring for several minutes.

Notes:

# AT HOME ON THE RANGE

# WANTED

*Recipes For When You Feel Like Cooking*

PICTURE YOURSELF LIVING IN THIS ECO-FRIENDLY, RUSTIC SOD HOME, FEATURING A LARGE EXPANSIVE YARD. INDOORS THERE'S A KITCHEN, BEDROOM, 3/8 BATH, DEN, AND DINING ROOM; ALL INCORPORATED IN AN OPEN, STRUCTURELESS LIVING AREA. NATURALLY DEEP SET WINDOWS AND DOORS. WALK ACCESSIBLE MAIN BATH; PROVIDES ULTIMATE IN PRIVACY. WALLS-ROOF-FLOORS OFFER ADDITIONAL GARDENING SPACE. LOCATION ALREADY ZONED FOR EARTHWORM/FISHBAIT DEVELOPMENT. CALL "JEB" FOR DETAILS.

## "Super Bull" Chowder

**1 pound country style pork sausage**
**2 stalks broccoli**
**4 potatoes**
**Water**
**4 cups milk**
**10 ounces sharp cheddar cheese**
**4 tablespoons flour or corn starch**
**1 1/2 teaspoons salt, or to your taste**

Brown sausage; drain off as much of the grease as possible. Add the broccoli and potatoes with water to cover. Simmer until vegetables are tender. Add the milk, reserving 1/4 cup in which you stir flour or corn starch. Add to pot with cut up cheese and the salt. Heat only until cheese melts and chowder thickens.

## Miss Jen's Beta Carotene Soup

29 ounce can pumpkin
6 large carrots
2 sweet potatoes
1 red pepper
2 onions
6 1/8 cups beef broth
1/2 cup chopped parsley
1 cup skim evaporated milk
2 teaspoons curry
Salt and pepper to taste

Cut up carrots, sweet potatoes, red pepper and onions. Add broth and heat to a boil. Reduce heat and simmer 30 minutes. Puree. Add pumpkin and cover. Bring back to a boil, reduce heat and simmer 15 minutes. Add curry, salt, pepper and milk. Stir and let stand for 10 minutes to let flavors blend. Note: For a change of pace, add two chopped, peeled apples with the vegetables.

## Shoo Fly Celery Soup

1 pound celery (1 heart with leaves plus 4 stalks)
1 medium onion (vidalia, if available)
1 quart chicken stock
1/2 stick butter
1 clove garlic
2 tablespoons Parmesan cheese
1/4 cup skim evaporated milk
Pepper
Thyme
2 tablespoons fresh parsley

Melt butter and cook onion, celery, garlic and parsley with it for 25 minutes in soup pot. Add stock and cook on medium heat for 25 minutes. Use hand blender to cream or puree vegetables. Add milk, cheese and seasonings.

## Bragger Jim's Best Pizza You Will Ever Eat

Crust:
1 cup warm water
1 tablespoon dry yeast
1 teaspoon honey
1 teaspoon salt
2 to 2 1/2 cups whole wheat flour

Sauce:
1/2 cup chopped onions
6 ounce can tomato paste
8 ounce can tomato sauce
1/2 teaspoon garlic salt
1/2 teaspoon oregano
1/4 teaspoon pepper

Toppings:
1/2 cup sliced ripe olives
1/4 cup sliced mushrooms
1/2 pound ground beef
1/2 pound mozzarella cheese
1/4 pound cheddar cheese

Mix together warm water, yeast and honey. Add salt plus 2 cups flour, adding more if needed. Let rise once; then smooth out in pan. Mix sauce ingredients together and heat. Spread sauce on dough. Add cheddar cheese and all other toppings, finishing off with the mozzarella cheese. Bake in moderately hot oven until cheese is melted and pizza is done.

## Painted Wagon Potato Salad Dressing

2 tablespoons flour
2 tablespoons sugar
1 teaspoon salt
1 teaspoon dry mustard
1/8 teaspoon paprika
1 egg, beaten
3/4 cup milk
1/4 cup vinegar
Celery salt
Chunk of butter

Blend flour, sugar, salt, mustard and paprika. Add egg, milk and vinegar. Cook over low heat until thickened. Remove from heat and add a few shakes of celery salt and a chunk of butter!

## Range Rider's Chow Mein

4 or 5 onions, chopped
1 package celery, sliced
1 1/2 pounds hamburger
1 1/2 pounds sausage
1 large can mushrooms
2 cans clear chicken broth
Cornstarch to thicken
Soy sauce
Cashews
Rice or noodles

Brown hamburger and sausage and drain. Add onions and celery and simmer for one hour. Add mushrooms, chicken broth and cornstarch. Simmer two hours. Serve over rice and noodles. Sprinkle with cashews and soy sauce as desired.

## Exotic Li'l Lyla's Lamb Curry

1 pound ground lamb
1 cup chopped onion
1 clove garlic, minced
2 teaspoons curry powder
2 medium tomatoes, peeled and chopped
1 medium apple, peeled and chopped
1/2 cup water
1 teaspoon instant bouillon granules
3/4 teaspoon salt
1/2 teaspoon ground ginger
1/4 cup cold water
1 tablespoon flour

Brown lamb, onion and garlic. Drain off any fat. Stir in curry powder and cook 1 minute. Stir in tomatoes, apple, water, bouillon, salt and ginger. Cover and simmer for 10 minutes. Combine the cold water with flour and stir into meat mixture, cooking until thickened. Serve over hot parsley rice (cook with chicken bouillon and add parsley) and pass condiments such as raisins, shredded coconut, chopped cucumber, chopped peanuts or crumbled bacon.

### *Marcia's Easy Burning Strudels*

**1 pound kielbasa, sliced, or**
   **2 to 3 cooked pork chops, chopped**
**1 can sauerkraut**
**1 loaf frozen bread dough, or**
   **use your favorite bread dough recipe**

Fry kielbasa or pork chop pieces in large fry pan. Add drained sauerkraut and cook until all starts to brown. Pat out the thawed dough as if you were making cinnamon rolls. Spread sauerkraut and kielbasa on the dough, roll up and seal. Slice as for rolls, 2 1/2 to 3 inches thick. Place a cup of liquid, water or a water and sauerkraut juice mix, plus a tablespoon of shortening in a heavy roaster. Set strudels in loosely. Partially cover and place in 350 degree oven. When browned nicely on the bottom, turn and finish baking. This will take approximately another 15 minutes. Add a little water if necessary. The original recipe calls for these to be made in a skillet on top of the stove, but Marcia always burned them!

### *Buffaloberry Jell*

**1 quart buffaloberries**
**3 quarts water**
**Sugar**
**Fruit pectin**

Boil berries and water until soft. Put through a jelly bag. Measure and use with fruit pectin and sugar according to package directions.

~~~~~~~~~~~~~~~~~~~~~~~~~~~~~~~~~~~~~~~~~

Traveling with Lewis and Clark through the prairies, Sacajawea would have seen the tiny bright berries that became known as buffaloberries. She was a Shoshoni Indian girl, pregnant and only 16 years old when she joined them. She deserves much credit for the survival and success of the expedition as she served as their guide and interpreter.

### Cooper's Steak & Sour Dough

**Round or sirloin steak**
**Flour seasoned with pepper and onion salt**
**Sour dough starter**
**Plain flour**

Pound out the steak, pounding in the seasoned flour. Dip pieces of steak in sour dough starter, then in plain flour. Fry until done in hot fat, preferably in a cast iron skillet. Serve with gravy.

### Simple Sour Dough Starter

**1 package yeast**
**4 cups flour**
**4 cups water**
**1 tablespoon sugar**

Combine ingredients and place in crock or jar. Let age. This will usually take several days to become bubbly and foamy. Refrigerate, adding equal parts of flour and water to replace any starter you remove.

# Ground Grizzly Jerky

**10 pounds ground venison or other game**
**1 cup soy sauce**
**2 tablespoons Worcestershire sauce**
**1 teaspoon black pepper**
**1 teaspoon garlic powder**
**1 teaspoon onion powder**
**1/2 teaspoon hot pepper sauce**
**4 ounces liquid smoke**

Mix liquid smoke and spices thoroughly with ground meat. Refrigerate over night. Line cookie sheets with waxed paper or use non-stick pans and cooking spray. Spread evenly with meat mixture to approximately 1/4 inch thickness. Bake at 150 degrees for 4 hours. Brush meat with water and turn occasionally while baking. While still soft, cut part way through to score in strips. Finish baking. Cool on racks. Break apart. Store in jars or plastic bags in the refrigerator. May be frozen.

## Jerry's Oyster-Oyster Stew

2 cans oysters
1 can smoked oysters
2 cups celery, chopped fine
1/2 cup chopped onions
Butter
Salt
Pepper
Milk
Evaporated milk or half and half
Hot pepper sauce

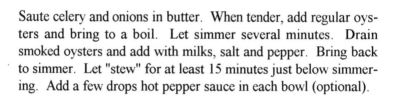

Saute celery and onions in butter. When tender, add regular oysters and bring to a boil. Let simmer several minutes. Drain smoked oysters and add with milks, salt and pepper. Bring back to simmer. Let "stew" for at least 15 minutes just below simmering. Add a few drops hot pepper sauce in each bowl (optional).

## Bellering Bull Green Chili Salsa

3 4-ounce cans chopped green chilies
8 pounds tomatoes, coarsely chopped
3 cups chopped onion
1 cup chopped bell peppers
1/4 cup lemon juice
6 tablespoons white vinegar
2 teaspoons oregano
1 tablespoon salt
Add if you want a hotter version:
  3 4-ounce cans Jalapeno peppers
  2 to 3 teaspoons crushed red peppers, or
  Red hot pepper sauce

Combine all ingredients and bring to a boil. Cover and simmer on low heat for 5 minutes. Put in jars and process 45 minutes in hot water bath. Make 8 pints.

## Bull Dogging BBQ Meatballs

**3 pounds ground beef**
**12 ounces evaporated milk**
**1 cup oatmeal**
**1 cup cracker crumbs**
**2 eggs**
**1/2 cup chopped onions**
**1/2 teaspoon garlic powder**
**1/2 teaspoon pepper**
**2 teaspoons salt**
**2 teaspoons chili powder**

Combine all ingredients and shape into balls. Place in a 13x9x2 pan. Pour on sauce (recipe below) and bake at 350 degrees for 1 hour.

Sauce:
**2 cups catsup**
**1 cup brown sugar**
**1/2 teaspoon liquid smoke**
**1/2 teaspoon garlic powder**
**1/4 cup chopped onion**

# ALONG the OLD WEST TRAIL

HONEST TO GOODNESS
## LEWIS & CLARK TRIVIA:
AMONG THE BOYS MANY
ACHIEVEMENTS; THEY WERE
THE VERY FIRST TO SEND A
SEATING PRESIDENT A
LIVE PRAIRIE DOG.

## Lewis and Clark Expedition

*Excerpts from* **Camp Pleasant Revisited** *by Hal Werner*

In 1803 Thomas Jefferson purchased the Louisiana Territory for $15 million. He commissioned William Clark and Merriwether Lewis to explore the Missouri River to the headwaters and then on to the Pacific Ocean. They provided the first written account of what they called "Camp Pleasant" and the surrounding area.

On May 14, 1804, a party of 45 departed from St. Louis up the Missouri. They traveled in one large boat and two peroques (flat bottom boats). They needed to carry supplies for the 2 1/2 year journey, plus sufficient goods for trading with the Indians along the way. They spent the first winter in a Mandan village in North Dakota and the second winter near the mouth of the Columbia River, returning back over the same trail to St. Louis in September of 1806.

Their journals are rich in descriptions of new lands, animals and plants. Descriptions from their journals told of new animals including prairie dogs, pronghorn antelope, jackrabbit, magpie, mule deer and coyotes. The prairie dog or barking squirrel, as Lewis and Clark called it, was first seen near what is now Ft. Randall (South Dakota) where the group spent the better part of a day trying to dig out, then drown out, specimens. They also called them ground rats. A bird never before seen in the Americas was killed near Corvus (crow) Creek. What later was identified as a magpie was called the American Crow and hence the name now used, American Crow Creek. They discovered the mule deer and would later call it that, as they did on their return trip in 1806 when they unsuccessfully tried to obtain a specimen for study. The party had seen what they called a fox or prairie wolf. Lewis later gives a complete description of what was the first account of the coyote. You are encouraged to explore the early Louisiana Territory through the journals of Lewis and Clark.

## Hal Makes Too Many Pancakes
### (Pancakes for Saddle Bums)

9 eggs
9 cups buttermilk
8 cups flour
3 teaspoons salt
4 1/2 teaspoons baking powder
4 1/2 teaspoons baking soda
1/2 cup sugar
1 cup oil

Combine above in a 5 quart ice cream pail.  Add milk to make the consistency you like.  You can add blueberries or serve with blueberry topping.

### Blueberry Topping

1/2 cup blueberries
2 tablespoons cornstarch
1 cup water
1 cup sugar

Dissolve the cornstarch in water.  Heat and simmer until thick.

## Back Woods Walleye Fish Fritters

**Walleye fillets cut in bite size pieces**
**Green pepper, chopped**
**Onions, chopped**
**Beer**
**Flour**
**Salt**
**Pepper**

Make up a beer batter using beer and flour, seasoned with salt and pepper. The batter should be thick, like the consistency of dumplings. Mix in the fish, green pepper and onions. Drop from a spoon into 375 degree oil and cook until golden brown.

~~~~~~~~~~~~~~~~~~~~~~~~~~~~~~~~~~~~~~~~~

Ron Schara acquired this recipe from a fishing guide that took him to the Lake of the Woods. Ron is a newspaper columnist for the Minneapolis Star Tribune and TV host for the show, "Minnesota Bound."

~~~~~~~~~~~~~~~~~~~~~~~~~~~~~~~~~~~~~~~~~

## Bro. David's Sour Cream Raisin Pie

1 baked pie crust (9" or 10")
1 1/2 cups raisins
1/2 cup water
1/2 cup sour cream
1/2 teaspoon cinnamon
1/2 teaspoon instant coffee
Dash of ground cloves
4 ounce box regular vanilla pudding
2 cups milk
2 egg yolks

Simmer raisins in the water. Steam in covered pan for 10 minutes. Remove from heat but do not drain. Stir in sour cream, cinnamon, instant coffee and cloves. Let cool slightly while you prepare the pudding. Prepare the pudding according to instructions on box with 2 cups of milk. When thick add the egg yolks. Cook until smooth and thick. Use double boiler for best results. Stir raisin and sour cream mixture into pudding and fill crust.

3 egg whites
1 teaspoon vanilla
1/2 cup sugar
1 teaspoon cream of tartar

Prepare meringue by beating egg whites to soft peaks. Gradually add the remaining ingredients and beat until stiff. Top pie filling, spreading to the edge. Brown in 350 degree oven.

~~~~~~~~~~~~~~~~~~~~~~~~~~~~~~~~~~~~~~~

The Sour Cream Raisin Pie recipe was developed by Bro. David Nagel, a member of the Congregation of the Priests of the Sacred Heart. For 11 years Bro. David was the Food Service Director at St. Joseph's Indian School, has served as Director of Development and currently is Executive Director. The recipe has received recognition as an outstanding dessert idea.

~~~~~~~~~~~~~~~~~~~~~~~~~~~~~~~~~~~~~~~

## Sunrise On The Cattledrive Coffee Cake

When you have to rise early for the annual cattledrive or an early morning hunt, make this up the night before and bake the next morning.

3/4 cup white sugar
3/4 cup brown sugar
3/4 cup butter
2 eggs, beaten
2 cups flour
1 teaspoon baking powder
1 teaspoon baking soda
1/2 teaspoon salt
1 1/2 teaspoons cinnamon
1 cup buttermilk
1 cup chopped nuts
1 cup brown sugar
1 teaspoon cinnamon

Cream first sugars and margarine. Beat in eggs. Add dry ingredients. Add the buttermilk and mix well. Pour into a greased pan. Mix together last cup of brown sugar, nuts and cinnamon and sprinkle on batter. Bake at 350 degrees 30 to 45 minutes.

~~~~~~~~~~~~~~~~~~~~~~~~~~~~~~~~~~~~~~~~

This is a recipe from Linda and Merrill of the Diamond Dot Ranch. Of course pheasant is their favorite cuisine! If you want great upland bird hunting, including the wily ringneck pheasant, prairie chicken, dove, partridge and sharp tail grouse, coupled with prairie and river break scenery and South Dakota hospitality, contact them at the Diamond Dot Ranch, HCR 5, Box 11, Reliance, SD 57569.

~~~~~~~~~~~~~~~~~~~~~~~~~~~~~~~~~~~~~~~~

## *Thunderstik Pheasant In Cream*

**4 pheasant breasts, skinned and boned**
**Flour, seasoned with salt and pepper**
**Butter and cooking oil**
**1/2 cup diced onion**
**1/2 cup diced celery**
**1 cup sliced fresh mushrooms**
**1 cup cream of mushroom soup**
**1 cup whipping cream**
**1/2 cup white wine**

Dust pheasant breasts in seasoned flour. Saute in half butter and half oil until lightly browned. Place in casserole dish. Make sauce by sauteing the onion, celery and mushrooms in butter. Add the soup, cream and wine. Blend together and pour over the pheasant. Bake covered in 300 degree oven for 2 hours. Serve with wild rice and sliced apples. Enjoy!

~~~~~~~~~~~~~~~~~~~~~~~~~~~~~~~~~~~~~~~~~~

The Pheasant In Cream recipe was shared with us by the Thunderstik Lodge, located a few minutes from Chamberlain, South Dakota. Thunderstik provides five star accommodations and premier customer service for a one of a kind hunting experience. In addition to pheasant hunting, they offer some of the best duck and goose hunts. And after the hunt you'll be able to unwind in the Sundowner Room which provides a relaxing atmosphere and a breathtaking view of the Missouri River.

~~~~~~~~~~~~~~~~~~~~~~~~~~~~~~~~~~~~~~~~~~

## Corn Bread with a Punch

1 cup all purpose flour
1 cup yellow cornmeal
1 tablespoon sugar
1 1/2 teaspoons baking powder
1/2 teaspoon baking soda
1 teaspoon salt
1 1/2 cups buttermilk
2 large eggs, beaten lightly
1 cup fresh corn, about 2 ears
3 tablespoons vegetable shortening, melted and cooled
1/4 cup sun dried tomatoes
3 Jalapeno peppers, seeded and chopped fine
Dash of cayenne pepper

Sift together flour, cornmeal, sugar, baking powder, baking soda and salt. Soak tomatoes in hot water for eight minutes, drain and chop fine. Don't use the tomatoes that are packed in oil. Stir together buttermilk, eggs, corn, shortening, tomatoes, Jalapeno peppers and cayenne pepper. Stir buttermilk mixture into flour mixture until just combined. Don't over mix. Pour batter into buttered 8 inch square (2 quart) glass baking dish. Bake on middle rack of oven 40 minutes at 375 degrees or until a tester comes out clean. Cool in dish on a rack for 10 minutes. Invert onto a cutting board, cut and serve.

~~~~~~~~~~~~~~~~~~~~~~~~~~~~~~~~~~~~~~~~~

We call Terry Hogan the "cheesecake man". He is owner and originator of The Original Temptation Co. that makes and distributes The Original Sensation Cheesecake Bar. He started cooking professionally while living in Essex, CT. He made his way from cooking on the Schooners sailing out of Old Mystic Seaport to Buckley House in New London, CT., to Mexico City. In Mexico he started "Simply the Best Cheesecakes" for the Americans living in the city of 30 million people. After 4 years he sold the company and moved back to Ohio. He started The Original Temptation Co. after moving to the Dakotas, and now resides at 204 Forrest Hill Drive, Tompkinsville, Ky 42167.

## Pheasant in Golden Sherry Creme Sauce

2 boneless pheasant breasts (West River select)
4 tablespoons flour
1/2 teaspoon white pepper
1/4 teaspoon paprika
4 tablespoons olive oil
2 tablespoons butter
1/2 teaspoon fresh chopped garlic
1/4 cup creme sherry
1 pint half and half cream
1 cup sliced mushrooms
Toasted almonds and fresh chopped parsley

Cut breasts in 4 pieces. Sift together the flour, pepper and paprika and use to dust pheasant pieces. Brown in the olive oil and butter with the garlic. Place in a baking dish. Deglaze the sauce pan with sherry and cream, adding the mushrooms and reducing to half. Pour over breasts and bake 20 minutes. Garnish with toasted almonds and fresh chopped parsley. Excellent with wild rice and carrots in browned butter and honey dill glaze.

(According to Cheryl, pheasants from the west banks of the Missouri are more flavorful--milo and grain select!)

~~~~~~~~~~~~~~~~~~~~~~~~~~~~~~~~~~~~~~~~

Cheryl Jordan comes from "Big Sky Country", Montana. She has been enjoying the "tastes" of her trade for 25 years. From her family restaurant, the gourmet room "Quentinellis," to banquet manager at Cedar Shore Resort at Chamberlain, SD, she has shared her cooking ideas, her cheese carved pheasants and special painted plate desserts featuring chocolate geese, bugling elk and pheasants.

~~~~~~~~~~~~~~~~~~~~~~~~~~~~~~~~~~~~~~~~

## *Trophy Buckle Banana Foster*

**Butter**
**Brown sugar**
**Bananas**
**1 shot of triple sec**
**1 shot of southern comfort**
**1 shot of creme de banana**
**1 shot of brandy**
**2 shots of 100 proof bacardi rum**
**Ice cream**
**Whipping cream**

Place butter in heated saute pan, blend with brown sugar and caramelize.  Add thinly sliced bananas (1 banana for 2 people). Add triple sec, southern comfort, creme de banana and brandy. Stir and add more brown sugar for thickness.  Add 1 shot of the rum, floated on top.  Add one shot of rum to serving ladle and heat until flaming.  Pour into sauce pan to create flame and stir until fire dissipates. Serve over ice cream.  Top with fresh whipping cream.

~~~~~~~~~~~~~~~~~~~~~~~~~~~~~~~~~~~~~~~~~

This recipe has been adapted from the original New Orleans recipe and has been used in many country clubs on the east coast. It was shared by Timothy Burrell.  He has worked in "food and beverage" at hotels and country clubs for 24 years.

~~~~~~~~~~~~~~~~~~~~~~~~~~~~~~~~~~~~~~~~~

TO DISCOURAGE ANTI-SOCIAL INTERPERSONAL EXCHANGES ..... COLORADO MINERS GAVE THEIR TOWN THE NAME:" FAIRPLAY."

AFTER YOU.'

NO, AFTER YOU.'

OOH! JUST SHOOT HIM!

## Sagebrush Pheasant Sausage

**Pheasant breast**
**Side pork or bacon**
**Seasoned flour**


Grind equal amounts of pheasant breast with side pork or bacon. This can then be made into patties. Roll them in flour that has salt and pepper added. Brown in a hot skillet on both sides. Turn down the heat and add 1/4 cup of water for each 8 patties. Let them cook slowly for at least 20 minutes. Edna says these are tasty with pancakes and homemade syrup.

~~~~~~~~~~~~~~~~~~~~~~~~~~~~~~~~~~~~~~

The Gunderson family owns and operates the G&C Pheasant Farm at Chamberlain, South Dakota. They work exceptionally hard raising the pheasants, actually starting with the eggs! The most enjoyable part of the year is fall when they provide hunters with excellent hunting plus a family atmosphere and great down-home cooking. Edna Gunderson shared this recipe that she serves to their hunters.

~~~~~~~~~~~~~~~~~~~~~~~~~~~~~~~~~~~~~~

## A True Pioneer - Grandma Gertrude
### Written by her daughter, Edith Werner

Gertrude McAnaly was born in 1879 in Hymera, Indiana, and came west to South Dakota to homestead and to teach school. Her homestead was in Gregory County near Dixon, but her first school was in Anoka, Nebraska. She came back on weekends to her claim shanty. The next year she taught school near her homestead, in a little shack. When her new school house was built, she and the "big boys" of the school loaded the benches, the stove and the books into "Teacher's Buggy" and moved into the school house. The books were all different. Each pupil brought what he had. Some of the pupils were of Bohemian background and did not speak English. By the next year, another school opened a few miles away and a young man from West Virginia was the teacher. Loyd had a four mile walk to court Gertrude. A year later they were married, and they raised a family of eight children.

## Grandma Harless's Mustard Ring

**4 eggs**
**1 cup water**
**1/2 cup vinegar**
**3/4 cup sugar**
**1/2 teaspoon tumeric**
**1 1/2 tablespoons mustard**
**1/4 teaspoon salt**
**1 envelope unflavored gelatin**
**1 cup heavy cream, whipped**

Beat eggs in top of double boiler. Add water and vinegar. Mix together balance of ingredients except cream and stir into egg mixture. Cook over boiling water until slightly thick. Set aside and let cool. Fold in whipped cream. Place in ring mold and refrigerate to set. This can be garnished to look very festive! Grandma ate this at a friend's house one Thanksgiving. It's great with a holiday meal.

*I shall grow old but never lose life's zest*
*Because the road's last turn will be the best*
*anon*

Bringing In The Scrap

WORDS BY
Mrs. Gertrude Harless

VERSE:

We are told that we must plant, 'tis no time to rave or

rant When they tell us we must save in ev - 'ry way

be it rub - ber, fats, or iron, we don't give a good gosh

darn We are bringing in the scrap to - day

Grandma Harless would have been in her sixties during World War II, a time when relations with the countries and people with whom we were fighting were very stressed. She did what she could for the war effort, from teaching all eight grades in a rural school on the Lower Brule Indian Reservation to writing this song.

## Settler's Easy Peach Pie

**Fresh sliced peaches**
**1 cup sugar**
**2 eggs**

Mix sugar and eggs with the peaches and put in unbaked pie crust. Bake at 425 degrees 35 to 40 minutes.

~~~~~~~~~~~~~~~~~~~~~~~~~~~~~~~~~~~~~~~

The times of the Old West were exciting and harsh. From the gun fights in the streets to the dance hall girls it was a time of action and adventure. Relive the days at the Old West Museum, Chamberlain, SD. Visit the main street and see the the cowboy and Indian displays. Be sure to see the colt revolving rifle and the woman's "hair care" section. Alice took time from her busy schedule at the Old West Museum to share her pie recipe with us.

~~~~~~~~~~~~~~~~~~~~~~~~~~~~~~~~~~~~~~~

# COUNTRY CLUB CUISINE

# WANTED

## "Country" Club Style Fixin's

## Cattle Guard Chicken

4 chicken breasts, with slit in middle
1 cup of sour cream
1 can condensed cream of mushroom soup
4 slices of bacon
4 slices of Swiss cheese
4 slices of corned beef

Place a slice of cheese and a slice of the corned beef in the chicken. Wrap with bacon. Marinate 24 hours in soup and sour cream. Bake at 325 degrees for 2 hours or until done.

## Cool As A Cucumber Salad

1 small package lemon gelatin
1 small package lime gelatin
1/2 teaspoon salt
1 1/2 cups boiling water
1 cup cold water
1 tablespoon vinegar
2 tablespoons lemon juice
1/4 cup mayonnaise
1/4 cup sour cream
1 small package cream cheese, softened
2 cups seeded cucumber, chopped
1/2 cup green onions, chopped
1/4 cup green pepper, chopped
1/4 cup sliced ripe olives

Dissolve gelatin in boiling water. Add cold water, vinegar, and lemon juice. Blend together the mayonnaise, cream cheese and sour cream and stir into gelatin mixture. When partially set, stir in vegetables. Chill until firm.

## Baxter's Spinach Salad

**Spinach greens**
**Mandarin oranges**
**Scallions, finely chopped**
**Candied almonds**

Make candied almonds by melting **1 tablespoon butter** with **2 tablespoons sugar** and adding **1/4 cup unblanched almonds.** Cook until sugar coats nuts.  Cool on wax paper.  Break nuts apart as you remove them from the paper.

Salad Dressing:
**1/4 cup oil**
**2 tablespoons sugar**
**2 tablespoons raspberry vinegar**
**1 tablespoon chopped parsley**
**Pepper**
**A few dashes of hot pepper sauce**

Shake well and pour over salad.

## Golden Hills Gourmet Potatoes

6 medium potatoes
1/4 cup butter
1/3 cup chopped green onions
3 cups shredded cheddar cheese
1 to 1 1/2 cups sour cream
Salt and pepper to taste

Cook potatoes in skins. Cool. Peel and shred coarsely. Combine cheese and butter in pan over low heat, stirring until almost melted. Remove from heat and blend in sour cream, onions, salt and pepper. Fold in potatoes and turn into greased casserole dish. Bake 25 minutes at 350 degrees.

## Rocky's Chicken Cordon Bleu

2 whole chicken breasts, boned and split in half
4 thin slices fully cooked, smoked ham
4 thin slices Swiss cheese
1/4 cup flour
1/4 teaspoon salt
1/4 teaspoon pepper
1 egg, slightly beaten
1/2 cup dry bread crumbs
3 tablespoons vegetable oil
2 tablespoons water

Flatten each piece of chicken breast to 1/4 inch thickness between plastic wrap or wax paper. Place a slice of ham and a slice of cheese on each piece. Roll up carefully, beginning at narrow end. Secure with wooden picks. Mix flour, salt and pepper. Coat rolls with flour mixture. Dip rolls into egg and roll in bread crumbs. Heat oil in skillet over medium heat. Cook rolls 10 minutes, turning occasionally until light brown. Add water. Cover and simmer about 10 minutes or until juices run clear. Remove picks and serve.

### Rattler Rice Salad

3 cups rice, cooked and cooled
Large box instant vanilla pudding
1 1/4 cups softened ice cream
3 teaspoons cinnamon
1 cup raisins, softened in boiling water
1 small tub frozen whipped topping, thawed

Mix ice cream and pudding together. Add all other ingredients; mix and chill.

### Becca's Arena Snack Crackers

1 bag oyster crackers
1 cup vegetable oil
1 package ranch style dressing mix
1 to 2 teaspoons garlic powder

Mix oil, dressing mix and garlic powder together and microwave for 1 minute. Pour oil mixture over crackers and stir until evenly covered with seasoning.

### Snickering Stable Boy's Salad

1 large box instant vanilla pudding
1 1/2 cups milk
1 small tub frozen whipped topping, thawed
2 king size chocolate peanut candy bars, chopped
2 large apples, chopped

Mix and chill.

## Coyote Cucumber Rice

**Rice**
**Chicken stock or bouillon**
**Cucumbers**

Cook rice using the chicken stock as liquid.   Meanwhile, peel cucumbers and slice lengthwise Remove seeds.   Fry in oil until they are tender and brown.   Place in rice.   Great with chicken. Just ask the coyote!

## Mexican Sunflower

**2 cups refried beans**
**1 cup Jalapeno dip**
**1 cup green onion dip**
**8 ounce package shredded cheddar cheese**
**1 medium tomato chopped**
**4 chopped green onions**
**1 small can sliced black olives**
**1 bag taco chips**

Layer ingredients in order listed.   Place chips around layered dip in layers making plate look like flowers.

## Green Horn Salad

**1/2 cup brown sugar**
**8 ounces sour cream**
**1 1/2 pounds whole green grapes**
**1 cup crushed pineapple, drained**
**8 ounce tub frozen whipped topping, thawed**
**1 cup walnut pieces**

Mix all ingredients and chill before serving.

## Gringo's Green Rice

2 cups cooked rice
1 large carton sour cream
2 cups shredded colby cheese
1 package frozen spinach, drained
2 cans green chilies, diced
1 teaspoon salt
Buttered bread crumbs

Mix together all ingredients except bread crumbs. Chop spinach
fine and make sure to squeeze out all liquid. Bake 1 hour at 350
degrees, adding buttered bread crumbs on top during the last 15
minutes.

## Gully Washer Golf Course Drink

1 cup cranberry juice cocktail
1 cup pineapple juice
1/2 cup orange juice
1 sliced banana
10 ice cubes

Place juices and banana in blender. Cover and blend on high,
adding ice through top.

## Yippee Yi Yeah Punch

1 small package strawberry gelatin
1 cup boiling water
1 package strawberry drink powder
2 quarts water
2 1/2 cups sugar
1 large can pineapple juice
1 bottle ginger ale
1 quart pineapple sherbet

Dissolve gelatin in hot water. Combine with other ingredients
except ginger ale and sherbet. Refrigerate to cool. When ready
to serve, add ginger ale and sherbet.

## Red Lake Casserole

1 1/3 cups quick cooking rice
1/3 cup slivered almonds
1/3 cup chopped onions
1 package frozen chopped spinach
2 cubes chicken bouillon
1/2 cup hot water

Cook rice according to directions. Fry almonds in butter. Then fry the onions. Thaw and wilt spinach in boiling water. Mix 1/2 of spinach, 1/2 of almonds and all of the onions and bouillon (dissolved in the 1/2 cup hot water) with rice. Place balance of spinach in bottom of casserole dish. Place rice mixture over this. Top with the rest of the almonds. Heat through, 20 to 30 minutes in 350 degree oven.

## Reuben's Potatoes

Bake **potatoes**. Split open. Pour in a small amount of **thousand island dressing**. Add **sauerkraut** and **corned beef**. Top with **Swiss cheese**. Broil until cheese melts. Sprinkle with **rye bread crumbs or croutons**.

## Teetotaler Cherry Coke Salad

2 large packages cherry gelatin
2 cups hot water
1 cola
1 can pineapple, drained
1 can bing cherries, drained
8 ounces cream cheese, softened
1 cup chopped nuts

Dissolve gelatin in hot water. Add cola plus enough juices from fruit to make right amount of cold liquid as specified in gelatin instructions. Add cream cheese and nuts. Stir again when starting to set.

## Covered Wagon Chicken

4 cups chicken, cubed
1 1/2 tablespoons lemon juice
3/4 cup mayonnaise
1 teaspoon seasoning salt
2 cups celery, finely chopped
1/2 cup ripe olives, sliced
2 hard boiled eggs, sliced
1 can cream of chicken soup
1/4 cup chopped green onions
1 cup grated cheese
3/4 cup chopped toasted almonds
1 1/2 cups "Vinegar and Salt" flavored
      potato chips, crushed*

Put all ingredients except nuts, cheese and potato chips in a large flat baking dish. Top with remaining ingredients. Let stand for several hours or overnight in refrigerator. Bake at 400 degrees for 25 minutes or until thoroughly heated and top is browning.

*Vinegar and salt flavored chips are available at most grocery stores.

## Neoma's Pony Express Casserole

2 cans mixed vegetables, drained
1 cup chopped onion
3/4 cup mayonnaise
1 can water chestnuts, chopped
1 cup shredded cheddar cheese
1 cup celery, sliced
1 roll Ritz crackers
Butter

Combine all items except crackers in a casserole dish. Crush crackers and saute in butter. Top casserole with cracker layer, then bake at 350 degrees for 30 minutes.

## Rodeo Rider's Turkey Rolls

**2 8-ounce packages crescent rolls**
**Butter**
**6 ounces cream cheese, softened**
**1 cup Monterey Jack cheese, grated**
**4 ounce can mushrooms, drained**
**2 cups chopped cooked turkey**
**Dill weed**
**1/2 cup finely chopped walnuts**
**1/2 cup dry bread crumbs**
**1/2 stick melted butter**

Flatten crescent rolls. Spread with thick layer of butter. Stir together cheese, turkey and mushrooms and spread on the crescent rolls. Sprinkle with dill weed. Roll up the crescent rolls. Mix together walnuts and crumbs. Dip each roll in melted butter and roll in crumbs. Bake 15 minutes at 400 degrees.

## Country Swing Salsa

1 large can Italian tomatoes or chopped
      fresh tomatoes to make 3 1/2 cups
1 can sliced ripe olives
1 can chilies, diced
1 green pepper, finely chopped
1 bunch green onions including tops, chopped
1 clove garlic, finely minced
Salt and pepper
A few shakes of hot pepper sauce!

## Headin' West Hawaiian Chicken

1/4 teaspoon ground ginger
4 cloves garlic, chopped fine
2 tablespoons soy sauce
Pineapple juice
1 can pineapple chunks, drained
1 chicken, cut up

Drain pineapple and refrigerate chunks. Use juice, ginger, garlic
and soy sauce to make a marinade for the chicken. Marinate at
least 1/2 day. Remove chicken, dry, roll in flour and brown in
shortening. Pour marinade mixture over chicken. Add pineapple
chunks. Boil mixture for short time. Put in oven for at least 1
hour at 325 degrees.

## Green Stuff Dip

2 avocados, mashed
Pepper and garlic salt
1/4 cup chopped onions
2 tablespoons chopped green chilies
2 tablespoons finely chopped tomato
1 tablespoon mayonnaise

Mix together. Add a few drops of **hot pepper sauce**, if desired.
If prepared ahead of time, add a little **lemon juice**.

## Creek Xing Chicken Wings

Chicken wings, deep fat fried

Sauce:
1/2 cup hot sauce
1/4 cup melted butter
3 tablespoons Worcestershire sauce
1/2 teaspoon garlic powder
1 teaspoon paprika
1 teaspoon crushed red pepper or use paprika (milder!)

Pour sauce over wings. Bake 1/2 hour at 375 or 1 hour at 350 degrees.

## Crabby Old Hen Wings

Chicken wings
1 cup soy sauce
1 cup brown sugar
3/4 cup water
1/4 cup vinegar
1 teaspoon dry mustard
1/2 teaspoon garlic powder

Brown chicken wings. Combine other ingredients and heat to simmer. Place wings in baking dish and pour sauce over them. Bake approximately 1 hour at 300 degrees. If you don't brown chicken wings, bake additional time until wings are tender and well done.

IRRATIONAL HISTORY:
BUFFALO WINGS AT ONE TIME BECAME SO POPULAR THE SPECIES WAS THREATENED.

## Wild Horse Charley's Casserole

1 1/2 pounds ground beef
1 onion, chopped
1 cup sliced mushrooms
2 cloves garlic, minced
1 cup diced green pepper
14 1/2 ounce can stewed tomatoes
8 ounce can tomato sauce
1/4 teaspoon basil
1/4 teaspoon salt
1/4 teaspoon pepper
1/8 teaspoon oregano leaves
2 cups cooked rice or pasta
1 cup grated cheddar cheese

Brown hamburger, drain, and set aside. Saute onion, mushrooms and garlic in vegetable oil until soft. Add green pepper and hamburger and saute for 5 minutes. Stir in tomatoes and seasonings and simmer for 15 minutes. Stir rice or pasta into mixture and spoon into casserole dish. Bake 20 to 25 minutes in 350 degree oven. Sprinkle on cheese. Broil 2 minutes or until cheese is lightly browned.

## Thundering Herd Fried Chicken

1 chicken, cut up
1 cup flour
2 teaspoons salt
1/4 teaspoon pepper
2 eggs
3 tablespoons milk
1 1/2 cups finely chopped, blanched almonds

Heat oven to 400 degrees. Melt a small amount of butter in the baking dish. Mix together flour, salt and pepper. Coat chicken with flour mixture, then dip in eggs beaten with the milk. Roll in almonds. Let stand 5 to 10 minutes. Place chicken skin side down in the melted butter. Bake 30 minutes, turn and bake until tender, approximately another 30 minutes.

## Break Away Brunch Taters

3 tablespoons butter
3 medium potatoes (unpeeled), boiled and diced
1 1/4 cups grated Monterey Jack Cheese
1 1/4 cups grated cheddar cheese
2/3 cup diced tomato
2 tablespoons minced onion
2 tablespoons chopped green onions
Salt
1/2 cup diced avocado
1/2 cup sour cream

Cook potatoes in butter until browned and crisp. Add remaining ingredients except avocado and sour cream and stir until cheeses are melted. Gently add avocado. Top with dollops of sour cream.

## Clownin' Creme Pie

1/2 cup slivered almonds, chopped
15 ounces sweetened condensed milk
1/3 cup lemon juice
1/2 teaspoon almond extract
1/3 cup heavy cream, whipped
1 can cherry pie filling

Use your favorite pie crust recipe, adding the almonds when you stir in the water. Bake crust as usual. Combine the milk, lemon juice and extract, stirring until mixture thickens. Fold in whipped cream. Top with cherry pie filling.

## Desperado Appetizer

8 ounces cream cheese
1/2 pint sour cream
1/2 packet taco seasoning
1 mashed avocado

Blend above, spread on plate and cover with chopped **lettuce, tomatoes, cheddar cheese** and **black olives**.

## Fancy Filly Pizza Puff

**White bread slices with crusts removed**
**12 ounces mozzarella cheese**
**6 ounce can tomato paste**
**1 tablespoon basil leaves**
**1 1/2 pounds pork sausage**
**3/4 teaspoon salt**
**5 eggs**
**3 cups milk**

Brown sausage and simmer 15 minutes. Drain well. Grease
9x13 pan and cover bottom with bread slices. Spread tomato
paste and basil on bread. Cover with 1/2 the cheese. Add the
sausage and then cover with remaining cheese. Quarter slices of
bread and make a top layer. Beat eggs, milk and salt and pour
over bread. Cover with plastic wrap and refrigerate overnight.
Bake 45 minutes at 350 degrees.

## Tumbleweed Tuna Balls

2 cups corn flakes, crushed
1/3 cup milk
1/4 cup mayonnaise
1 can tuna, drained
1/4 cup minced onion
1 tablespoon parsley
1/2 teaspoon Worcestershire sauce
1 teaspoon lemon juice
1/4 teaspoon salt
1/8 teaspoon pepper

Mix 1 cup cereal with milk. Add rest of ingredients and mix well. Form into 1 inch balls. Roll in balance of cereal. Place on well greased cookie sheet. Bake 10 to 15 minutes at 425 degrees.

## Mustang Mandarin Salad

1/4 cup sliced almonds
2 tablespoons sugar
Lettuce
2 medium stalks celery, chopped
2 green onions, including tops, chopped
1 can mandarin oranges, drained

Dressing:
1/4 cup vegetable oil
2 tablespoons sugar
2 tablespoons vinegar
1 tablespoon chopped parsley
1/2 teaspoon salt
Dash of pepper
Dash of red pepper sauce

Cook almonds and sugar over low heat until sugar is melted and almonds are coated. Cool and break apart. Make up salad of lettuce, celery, onions and oranges. Combine dressing ingredients and pour over salad mixture. Top with almonds.

## Levi's Stuffed Steak Rolls

2 pounds round steak
1 package seasoned stuffing croutons
1 medium onion, chopped fine
1 large can mushrooms
2 packages bleu cheese
1 beef bouillon cube
2 cups hot water

Cut steak into serving size pieces. Pound steak well. Mix croutons with onion, mushrooms and bleu cheese. Moisten with enough of the hot water, in which bouillon cube was dissolved, to make a stiff consistency stuffing. Place several spoonfuls across the steak pieces. Roll steak, fastening with toothpicks. Brown rolls in cooking oil. Place in casserole dish, add balance of bouillon/water mixture and cover. Bake in 350 degree oven until tender, approximately 1 1/2 hours.

## Fr. John's Canyon Creek Cheese Log

1 pound processed cheese spread, softened
8 ounces cream cheese, softened
1 small can chopped green chilies
1 small can chopped black olives
1 small jar diced pimento

On waxed paper, spread processed cheese to a rectangle 10x18 using a rolling pin and/or fingers. Place in refrigerator to firm up, approximately 45 minutes. Spread with cream cheese and top with chilies, olives and pimento. Looks like a pizza at this point. Using the wax paper which is under all of this, fold long edges of rectangle to center, overlapping slightly. Cover with more wax paper and return to refrigerator to firm up again. When ready to serve, turn over on a long platter, seam side down on dish or cut in half and turn over on two smaller platters. Practice makes perfect, and it is worth it. Truly a winner with everyone. Serve with crackers.

## Coming Round The Mountain Salad

1 large package lime gelatin
1 large package lemon gelatin
2 cups boiling water
1 can lemon flavored pop
1 can fruit cocktail or salad fruits
1 cup green grapes
6 sliced bananas
2 cups miniature marshmallows
1 package lemon pudding, instant
1 cup cream, whipped, or use whipped topping

Dissolve gelatins in water. Cool to lukewarm before adding pop
and can of fruit cocktail. When partially set, stir and then add
bananas and marshmallows. Set until firm. Make up pudding
and fold in the whipped topping. Use to frost salad.

## Sweat Lodge Salsa

10 ounces canned tomatoes (crushed)
3 tablespoons lemon juice
5 to 10 Jalapeno peppers, minced
1 large onion, minced
4 stocks celery, minced
3 tablespoons hot pepper sauce
1 tablespoon salt
4 tablespoons dried parsley flakes
1 tablespoon chili powder
1 tablespoon cumin
1 tablespoon garlic powder
1 tablespoon oregano
1 bunch green onions, minced
15 ounce can tomato sauce
6 ounce can tomato sauce
15 ounces spaghetti sauce
4 ounce can tomato sauce

Mix. Store in a jar. This gets hotter as it sets.

## The Gambler's Bourginon Beef

1 tablespoon butter
1 large onion, chopped
2 cans mushrooms
1 1/2 pounds round steak, sliced against grain
1 teaspoon salt
1/4 teaspoon marjoram
1/4 teaspoon thyme
1/8 teaspoon pepper
1 1/2 tablespoons flour
3/4 cup beef broth
1 1/2 cups red burgundy wine

Saute onions with mushrooms in butter until tender. Remove and
drain. Add meat to skillet and brown, adding oil if necessary.
Remove from heat. Sprinkle seasonings over meat. Mix flour
with broth and stir into skillet. Heat to boiling, stirring constantly. Boil and stir for 1 minute. Stir in wine. Cover and
simmer 1 hour or until meat is tender. (Liquid should always
cover meat. If necessary add more liquid, using 1 part broth to 2
parts wine.) Gently stir in onions and mushrooms; cook uncovered 15 minutes. Serve over hot rice.

**NOUVELLE
CUISINE**

**CAMPFIRE
CHOW**

## Farrier Fruit Pizza

Crust:
**1 1/2 cups flour**
**1/2 cup powdered sugar**
**1 stick plus 2 tablespoons margarine**

Filling:
**8 ounces cream cheese**
**8 ounces frozen whipped topping**
**1/2 cup powdered sugar**

Fruit:
**Your choice!**

Glaze:
**1 cup pineapple juice**
**1/2 cup sugar**
**2 1/2 tablespoons cornstarch**

Mix crust ingredients together and press into a jelly roll pan. Bake 7 to 8 minutes at 350 degrees. Beat filling items together and spread over cooled crust. Arrange fruits such as pineapple, strawberries and grapes on filling. Combine juice, sugar and cornstarch and cook until clear over medium heat. Cool and spread over fruits.

## Tuff's Vegetable Pizza

**2 packages crescent rolls**
**8 ounces cream cheese**
**1 package dry ranch dressing mix**
**1/3 cup mayonnaise**
**1 teaspoon dill weed**
**1 teaspoon parsley flakes**
**Fresh vegetables**

Pat dough together and flatten on a cookie sheet. Bake at 350 degrees for 10 to 12 minutes. Cool before adding topping. Cream together balance of ingredients except vegetables. Spread over crust. Top with chopped or grated vegetables such as broccoli, cauliflower, carrots, mushrooms, peppers, onions, celery, radishes and olives.

CONTRARY TO COMMON BELIEF; COWBOYS DIDN'T USE PROFANITY.

# Have a Ho Ho Hoe Down Holiday

# WANTED
## Ho Ho Hoedown Christmas Recipes

I was pleased to find I had saved a letter Tracy wrote to Santa when she was in grade school. She had a variety of interests and requests--and asked for some "delicious" things in her stocking!

Dear Santa Claus,

I would like a tape player or a recorder, a pizza maker and a basketball, an alarm clock and maybe a new pair of ice skates for later. Also the game Jaws and Pokeno.

I wish I had my old watch that I lost or a new one like it. Someday I'd like a mini-bike; even now, maybe. Maybe a bee-bee gun for in the summer.

In my stocking I would like a package of Philadelphia cream cheese and some other things like film for my camera, a pair of gloves to feed with, a package of banana bread, new cards, and tapes for the tape player or just tape for the recorder.

If you would like cookies, they are in containers on the table.

I'd like a gumball machine or someday a telephone in my room, a pocket fisherman and, for our family, a snow mobile for some day.

Love, Tracy Vaad

Merry Christmas, Merry Xmas, Santa Claus

## Horse Peddler Salad

1 large package red gelatin
1 can whole berry cranberry sauce
3 ounce package cream cheese, softened
1 1/2 cups whipped topping, thawed
1 cup pecans halves or pieces
Butter and salt

Make up gelatin as per directions only reduce cold water by one cup. Add can of cranberries. Stir when partially set to distribute cranberries. Toast pecans in small amount of butter in skillet until coated and starting to brown. Sprinkle salt over nuts and stir. Combine cream cheese and whipped topping. Frost when firm and sprinkle with pecans.

## Wrangler's Cranberry Punch

1 can jellied cranberries
1 can cranberry sauce
2 cups sugar
1 can frozen lemonade
1 can frozen orange juice
4 cups water
Lemon lime soda

Combine all except soda and freeze to a slush. Add soda and serve.

## Slippery Stirrup Salad

2 small packages lemon gelatin
3 cups boiling water
1/2 cup red hots
2 cups unsweetened applesauce
1 tablespoon lemon juice
Dash of salt
1/2 cup walnuts, chopped
2 small packages cream cheese, softened
1/4 cup milk
2 tablespoons mayonnaise

Dissolve gelatin and red hots in water. Stir in applesauce, lemon juice and salt. When partially set, add walnuts. Pour into 8x8x2 dish. Combine cream cheese, milk and mayonnaise. Spoon on top and marble through gelatin with spoon. Refrigerate to set.

## Stockyard Strength Wassail

6 cups apple cider
18 ounce can pineapple juice
4 cinnamon sticks
1/3 teaspoon nutmeg
1 1/2 teaspoons whole cloves
1 cup sugar, optional
1 tablespoon lemon peel
1/2 cup lemon juice
2 cups canned orange juice*
Lemon slices or wedges
Orange slices or wedges

Heat cider with cinnamon, nutmeg and cloves, simmering 5 minutes. Stir in sugar until dissolved, then stir in remaining ingredients, except lemon and orange slices. Simmer (very slowly, not letting it quite bubble or boil) additional 5 minutes. Float lemon and orange slices on top.

*Use canned juice as frozen juice has pulp.

## *Little Johnnie's Gumdrop Fruit Cake*

1 pound raisins
1 to 2 pounds gumdrops, cut ( don't use the black gumdrops)
1 cup pecans
4 1/2 cups flour
1 teaspoon cinnamon
1/4 teaspoon cloves
1/4 teaspoon nutmeg
2 eggs
1 teaspoon vanilla
1 cup butter
1 teaspoon baking soda dissolved in
      1 or 2 tablespoons hot water
2 cups sugar
2 cups applesauce

Sift dry ingredients together.  Use part of flour to dredge raisins, nuts and gumdrops.  Cream butter and sugar.  Add well beaten eggs.  Alternate adding flour and applesauce. Add soda (dissolved), vanilla,  raisins, nuts and gumdrops. Bake 2 hours at 300 to 325 degrees in waxed paper lined pans.

## "Women Of The West" White Fruit Cake

**2 cups butter**
**2 cups sugar**
**6 eggs**
**4 cups sifted flour**
**1 pound white raisins**
**1 pound pecans**
**1/2 pound glazed cherries**
**1/2 pound glazed pineapple**
**1 bottle lemon extract (1 1/2 ounce size)**

Lemon extract is the only liquid required in this cake. Cream butter and sugar. Add eggs one at a time and beat thoroughly after each addition. Dredge fruit in 1/2 cup of the flour and add the remaining portion to butter, sugar and egg mixture. Add nuts, fruit and lemon extract. Pour in well greased and floured pans. Place pieces of candied fruit on top for decoration. Tie a piece of heavy brown paper over the top of the pans for at least 30 minutes. Makes three cakes or bake in one large pan. Bake 1 to 1 1/2 hours in 300 degree oven, depending on the size of your pans.

# BELLY UP TO THE BAR

# WANTED

*Food With Spirits*

## Drifting Cowboy Black Bean Soup With Rum

2 cups chopped onion
1 cup chopped celery
1 clove garlic, diced fine
6 sprigs of parsley
2 sprigs of thyme or 1/4 teaspoon dried, crumbled
1 bay leaf
3 tablespoons unsalted butter
1 1/4 pounds ham hock
2 cups dried black beans
1 tablespoon packed brown sugar
6 cups beef broth
1/3 cup dark rum
Lemon juice to taste
Chopped hard boiled eggs

Pick over beans and soak covered in cold water over night. Drain. In a heavy kettle cook the onion, celery, parsley, thyme, garlic and bay leaf in the butter over moderately low heat, stirring for 10 minutes. Add ham hock, beans, brown sugar, broth and 4 cups water. Season with salt and pepper to taste. Bring the mixture to a boil, reduce the heat and simmer the mixture, uncovered, adding more water if necessary to keep the beans covered for three hours. Discard the ham hock and bay leaf. Put the mixture through the medium disk of a food mill into a large bowl and return it to the kettle. Stir in the rum, lemon juice and more salt and pepper to taste. Thin the soup to the desired consistency with hot water. Serve it with the chopped eggs for garnish.

Note: You may want to serve Terry's black bean soup with his corn bread recipe found in the <u>Along The Old West Trail</u> section.

## "*Brand*" ied *Beef*

**1/4 cup butter**
**3 pounds cubed beef**
**2 teaspoons orange peel**
**1/4 cup orange juice**
**1/4 cup bouillon**
**1/4 cup brandy**
**1 clove garlic, minced**
**1 large onion, cut in rings**

Brown butter in heavy skillet.  Add beef and cook until cubes start to brown.  Add remaining ingredients with the onion rings on top.  Cover and simmer over low heat or place in oven for at least 1 1/2 hours or until tender.  Cooking time may differ due to the cut of beef.

## Wewela Chuck Roast

**2 to 3 pound roast**
**1 cup cooking wine**
**1 package onion soup mix**
**1 can mushroom or celery soup**

Mix wine and onion soup mix together. Use as a marinade for roast, refrigerating over night. Remove roast, dry, then brown in Dutch oven, using small amount of cooking oil. Add marinade mix plus can of soup. Cover and simmer for 2 hours or until tender. Good served with wine sauce.

Wine sauce:
**1 tablespoon butter**
**1 tablespoon flour**
**1 cup beef bouillon**
**1/3 cup sweet red wine**

Combine and heat to simmer. Great with roast beef.

## Denim & Lace Punch

**One half of one fifth southern comfort**
**6 ounces fresh lemon juice**
**6 ounce can frozen lemonade**
**6 ounce can frozen orange juice**
**3 quarts lemon-lime soda**

Mix in punch bowl, adding soda last. Add red food coloring, if desired. Float ice block and orange and lemon slices.

## Bushwhacker Brats

**Bratwurst**
**Onions, sliced**
**1 can beer**

Place brats in heavy skillet. Cover with onions. Pour beer over brats and onions and simmer until no liquid remains. Turn brats, watching carefully that this doesn't start to burn. They will brown nicely and have a great flavor.

## Blue Sky Cheese Ball

8 ounces bleu cheese
8 ounces cream cheese
1 cup finely chopped celery
1/2 cup chopped walnuts
2 tablespoons whiskey

Mix together, form into ball and chill.

## Riverbreak Muffins

4 cups baking mix
3 tablespoons sugar
1 can beer
Brown sugar

Mix all together except brown sugar. Put in muffin tins and sprinkle with brown sugar. Bake 20 minutes at 350 degrees.

## Beer Butte Bread

3 cups self rising flour
3 tablespoons sugar
12 ounce can beer
2 tablespoons butter, melted
1/4 teaspoon garlic powder

Mix together flour, sugar and beer. Put in greased loaf pan and pour butter mixed with garlic powder over top. Bake in 375 degree oven for approximately 40 minutes.

## Prairie Onion Soup

4 to 6 sliced onions
1 teaspoon garlic powder
1/4 cup butter
2 tablespoons flour
4 cups beef bouillon
1 cup dry white wine
1 teaspoon Worcestershire sauce
1/2 teaspoon salt
1/4 teaspoon pepper
Croutons
Parmesan cheese

Brown onions in butter with garlic powder. Add flour and bouillon and cook ten minutes. Stir in wine and seasonings. Serve with croutons and parmesan cheese on top.

## Tipsy Bean Pot

Bacon strips
32 ounces baked beans
1 teaspoon dry mustard
1/4 cup molasses
1 onion, minced
1/4 cup blended whiskey

Mix together all items except bacon. Line your bean pot or dish with bacon strips. Carefully pour in bean mixture. Top with more bacon strips. Bake 1 hour in 325 degree oven.

## Jack Pot Chicken Breast

6 chicken breasts
1 cup sour cream
1 can mushroom soup
1/2 cup white wine
1 can sliced mushrooms

Place chicken in baking pan. Mix together sour cream, soup, wine and mushrooms. Pour over chicken breasts. Bake 1 hour to 1 1/4 hours at 350 degrees until tender and lightly browned. Serve with cucumber and rice dish found in the "Country" Club Cuisine section.

## Suet Pudding with Saucy Sauce

1 cup suet, cut fine
1 cup molasses
1 cup milk
3 cups flour
1 teaspoon baking soda
1/2 cup raisins
1 1/2 teaspoons salt
1/2 teaspoon ginger
1/2 teaspoon cloves
1/2 teaspoon nutmeg
1 teaspoon cinnamon
1/2 cup currants

Mix all ingredients together and put into glass or metal containers (makes 3 1-pound coffee tins). Steam for 3 hours.

Saucy sauce:
Make a simple sauce by heating a can of **vanilla frosting** and adding either **rum** or **rum extract** to taste.

## Bar Maid Creme De Menthe Cake

**White cake mix, prepared**
**3 tablespoons creme de menthe**
**1 can fudge topping**
**1 package frozen whipped topping**
**3 tablespoons creme de menthe**

Mix cake mix according to directions, adding the first creme de menthe. Bake as directed. While warm pour the fudge topping over the cake. Cool before frosting with the whipped topping combined with creme de menthe. Refrigerate until served.

## Dee's Home Brewed Beer Cake

**3/4 cup butter**
**2 cups sugar**
**2 eggs**
**1/2 cup cocoa**
**2 3/4 cups flour**
**2 teaspoons baking soda**
**1 cup beer**
**3/4 cup buttermilk**
**1/4 cup cherry juice**
**Jar of maraschino cherries, chopped**
**1 cup walnuts, chopped**

Cream butter and sugar. Add eggs and beat. Beat in the cocoa, flour and soda. Add beer, buttermilk and cherry juice. Stir in cherries and walnuts. Bake in 9x13 pan 40 to 45 minutes at 350 degrees.

# ReCiPeS fRom the PaCK HoRSE

# WANTED

*Food to "Store Up"*

## Sawyer's Soy Sauce Substitute

1 1/2 cups boiling water
4 tablespoons cider vinegar
4 tablespoons beef bouillon
1 tablespoon dark molasses
1 tablespoon oil

Mix all ingredients together. Keep refrigerated in a covered jar.

## Rustic Refrigerator Cucumbers

Cucumbers and onions, sliced
4 cups sugar
4 cups vinegar
1/2 cup salt
1 1/3 teaspoons tumeric
1 1/2 teaspoons celery seed
1 1/3 teaspoons mustard seed

Stir together pickling solution. Pour cold over cucumbers and onions in jars. Leave 5 days before eating. Will keep in refrigerator for 9 months.

## Cowpie Cucs

1 quart thinly sliced cucumbers
1 medium onion, sliced
1 tablespoon pickling salt
3/4 cup sugar
1/4 cup vinegar

Sprinkle salt over cucumbers and onion. Let stand at least one hour. Drain well. Mix together sugar and vinegar. Pour over cucumbers, mixing thoroughly. Freeze in small packages. Let thaw before serving.

### Corabelle's Cream Soup Substitute

2 cups nonfat dry milk
3/4 cup cornstarch
1/4 cup chicken bouillon crystals
2 tablespoons dried onion
1/4 teaspoon pepper
1 teaspoon thyme

Use 1/3 cup mix with 1 1/4 cups water as a substitute for a can of soup in your casserole.

### Grain Bin Granola

4 1/2 cups quick cooking oatmeal
2 cups wheat germ
2 tablespoons brown sugar
1 cup coconut
1/2 cup honey
1/3 cup salad oil
1 teaspoon vanilla
1 cup raisins
1 cup almonds

Mix together uncooked oatmeal, wheat germ, brown sugar and coconut. Stir in honey. Mix vanilla into salad oil and pour over above ingredients. Stir in raisins and almonds. Bake at 375 degrees for 20 minutes, stirring several times.

### Rising Moon Hot Chocolate Mix

1 cup powdered sugar
1 cup powdered creamer
8 cups dry milk powder
1 cup cocoa
1 vanilla bean, optional

Mix all ingredients together. Storing with a vanilla bean in the container gives this a gourmet taste. Add 1/3 cup mix to 1 cup boiling water.

## Calamity Jane's Sweet and Sour Dressing

1/2 cup flour
3/4 cup sugar
3 eggs, beaten
3/4 cup vinegar
1/8 teaspoon salt
2 cups water
1 cup oil

Mix together flour and sugar. Add all ingredients except oil. Cook until thick. Add oil and cook for several more minutes.

~~~~~~~~~~~~~~~~~~~~~~~~~~~~~~~~~~~~~

My Mother found Calamity Jane very interesting and told me this about her:

Jane made her way through the West from 1848 to 1903, often disguised as a man. She tramped along when the Union Pacific railroad was being built. Although a good shot, she wasn't an outlaw. Calamity served as an army teamster and worked as a nurse during the 1870 smallpox epidemic in the Dakotas. She died a poor woman in Deadwood, South Dakota, and was buried there next to Wild Bill Hickok.

~~~~~~~~~~~~~~~~~~~~~~~~~~~~~~~~~~~~~

## Open Range Baking Mix

**6 cups flour**
**1 cup dry milk powder**
**1/2 cup sugar**
**2 tablespoons baking powder**
**2 teaspoons salt**
**3/4 cup shortening**

Combine dry ingredients, then cut in shortening.

Pancakes:  **1 cup mix, 1 cup water and 1 egg**
Biscuits:  **1 cup mix and 1/3 cup water**

INSPIRED BY TALES OF WESTERN PROSPERITY;
MANY PIONEERS MOVED WEST IN WAGONS
LADEN WITH FURNITURE, FOOD, CLOTHING, TOOLS,
AND FAMILY....

I SAY WE LIGHTEN THE LOAD...

LET'S DUMP GRANDMA

## Tree Grove Teriyaki Sauce

1/2 cup soy sauce
1/4 cup salad oil
2 tablespoons molasses
2 teaspoons ginger
2 teaspoons dry mustard
4 cloves garlic, finely minced

Bring just to simmering while stirring. Cool and store in refrigerator.

## River Ranch Style Dressing

1 pint mayonnaise
1 pint buttermilk
1 1/2 teaspoons garlic powder
1 1/2 teaspoons onion powder
1 tablespoon parsley flakes
1/2 teaspoon black pepper
1 1/2 teaspoons salt

Combine and refrigerate.

## Chet Aching's Salad Dressing

1/4 cup brown sugar
3 tablespoons water
1 1/2 teaspoons celery seed
1/2 teaspoon paprika
2 1/2 tablespoons lemon juice
1 tablespoon Worcestershire sauce
1 tablespoon vinegar
1 cup salad oil
1/2 cup catsup
1/4 cup onion, minced

Cook sugar and water to soft ball stage. Cool. Liquefy balance of ingredients in blender. Turn blender to low and slowly pour in sugar mixture. Chill.

## Vinegar & Weeds

**2 cups vinegar**
**1 teaspoon herbs**

Make a flavored vinegar by combining it with the herbs.  Boil 1
minute, cover and let steep.  Store in a jar in the refrigerator.

## All Shook Up Coating Mix

**1 cup oil**
**2 tablespoons paprika**
**4 teaspoons salt**
**2 teaspoons celery salt**
**2 teaspoons pepper**
**2 teaspoons onion salt**
**2 teaspoons poultry seasoning**
**8 cups bread crumbs**

Or:
**1 cup flour or use half flour/half cornmeal\***
**1 teaspoon paprika**
**1 teaspoon salt**
**1/2 teaspoon pepper**
**1/2 teaspoon onion salt**
**1/4 teaspoon garlic salt**

The mixes are great for chicken, pork chops, veggies, etc.  Dip in
milk or other liquid before rolling in mix.  Can be placed in a
plastic bag with items you want to coat--just shake!

\*good for use on fish

# PET FOOD

# WANTED

*Pet Food*

## Bird "Feeders"

**Pine cone**
**Wire or strong string**
**Peanut butter**
**Milo, millet or prepared bird seed**

Fasten wire or string firmly around pine cone to use as the hanger. Spread with peanut butter, leaving some of the tips free so that birds have some "footing". Sprinkle with the seeds or press them into the peanut butter. Now enjoy the bird watching!

## Kitty's Catnip

**Catnip (mint)**
**Strong fabric**

I have been told that cats will eat fresh catnip, but it makes them act "weird"! It would probably be wise to dry the catnip and sew it into a pouch made from a strong fabric. Kitty can enjoy it without acting in an undesirable fashion!

## Dog Biscuits

1/4 cup warm water
1 tablespoon dry yeast
1 pint liquid (broth, milk, water)
8 1/2 cups flour, oatmeal and cornmeal (best if a combination
          of whole wheat, rye, oatmeal, cornmeal and regular
          flour)
2 cups sugar
1/2 cup dried milk (increase if liquid used is water)
2 teaspoons salt
1 egg
1 tablespoon water

Dissolve yeast in water and add to liquid. Add all other ingredients except egg and 1 tablespoon water. Knead dough and roll thin. Cut with cookie cutters and place on cookie sheets. Brush with egg beaten with water. Bake in 300 degree oven for 40 minutes. Let air dry before storing.

Note: Cook an extra ear of corn on the cob. Dogs love to chew on these--good substitute for bones.

## Reindeer Feed

Oatmeal
Cracked corn
Bird seed

Sprinkle the above mixture on deck, porch or wherever the reindeer usually park. They will eat what they like while Santa visits, and the birds can clean up the rest on Christmas Day.

## Horse Treats

Apples
Carrots

My mother's family raised Shetland ponies, and I grew up riding "Trixie" and "Star". They and our wonderful sorrel named Polly would have all voted for apples and carrots as favorite treats.

# Saddle Sores and Rawhide

# WANTED

*Remedies and Other "Stuff"*

## PIONEERS MAKING EARLY ATTEMPT AT LIGHTER THAN AIR TRAVEL.

Does your home need a little TLC?  Here is a recipe for a happy home:
Take equal parts of **cheerfulness** and **thoughtfulness** and **tact**. Season well with **contentment** and **unselfishness**.  Mix thoroughly with the milk of **human kindness** and add enough **common sense** to hold all together.  Serve on crisp leaves of a **sense of humor**.  This is a tested recipe that you are encouraged to share.

Roll pastry in one direction, turning the crust  instead of switching directions.

Brighten your silverware by soaking in your hot potato water.

To remove household odors, place a little vinegar in a pot of water and simmer.

Feet aching?  Apply a generous coating of petroleum jelly.  Pull socks up over this.  Sit back and relax with your feet on an electric heating pad.  You should feel better shortly!

Would you like to be able to eat more beans?  Here are some hints from Edna on making *Breakaway Beans.*
When I make my bean soup, I use **navy beans**.  Bring them to a rolling boil, adding 1/8 teaspoon of **ginger** and a teaspoon of **soda**.  This will really boil up; there goes the gas.  Rinse them very good, adding fresh water and a **ham bone** or meat from a picnic ham.  **Salt** and **pepper** to taste.  I add plenty of **onion** to my bean and potato soups.  I always dice the onion, cover  it with water and bring to boil.  Pour off the water,  which contains an oil that makes onion hard for some folks to digest.

If you are ever around someone who is choking, you will be very glad to know how to use the Heimlich Maneuver:

If choking occurs when food or other item becomes lodged in the windpipe, the person can die within several minutes time as they are not able to breathe. Stand behind the person and wrap your arms around their waist. Make a fist with one of your hands, grasping it with the other hand. Place this, thumb side toward the victim, on the abdomen just above the navel but below the rib cage. Give a sharp upward thrust with your fists. Repeat if necessary, but do be careful not to injure the person. If the victim is lying down on their back, you can apply this pressure by straddling the person and using the same pressure as above.

Soothe a sunburn by applying a soda and water paste or by placing cloths soaked in vinegar on the burn.

Put a tablespoon of vinegar in your fat before you deep fat fry, and your food will not be as greasy.

If you are cleaning wild ducks or geese, remove the down by dipping in or brushing on melted paraffin. Let it harden and when it is removed the down and pin feathers will come off with the wax.

Eggs can be kept for a year if stored in a quart of salt and a pint of slaked lime mixed in 3 gallons of water.

If you would like a lump free gravy, stir the flour into the melted fat. Then add cold liquid all at once. Stir vigorously.

Can't open the medicine bottle? Remember this formula: righty, tighty; lefty, loosey.

## Abbreviations for States

| | | | |
|---|---|---|---|
| Alabama | AL | Montana | MT |
| Alaska | AK | Nebraska | NE |
| Arizona | AZ | Nevada | NV |
| Arkansas | AR | New Hampshire | NH |
| California | CA | New Jersey | NJ |
| Colorado | CO | New Mexico | NM |
| Connecticut | CT | New York | NY |
| Delaware | DE | North Carolina | NC |
| District of Columbia | DC | North Dakota | ND |
| Florida | FL | Ohio | OH |
| Georgia | GA | Oklahoma | OK |
| Guam | GM | Oregon | OR |
| Hawaii | HI | Pennsylvania | PA |
| Idaho | ID | Puerto Rico | PR |
| Illinois | IL | Rhode Island | RI |
| Indiana | IN | South Carolina | SC |
| Iowa | IA | South Dakota | SD |
| Kansas | KS | Tennessee | TN |
| Kentucky | KY | Texas | TX |
| Louisiana | LA | Utah | UT |
| Maine | ME | Vermont | VT |
| Maryland | MD | Virginia | VA |
| Massachusetts | MA | Virgin Islands | VI |
| Michigan | MI | Washington | WA |
| Minnesota | MN | West Virginia | WV |
| Mississippi | MS | Wisconsin | WI |
| Missouri | MO | Wyoming | WY |

## Can Sizes

Picnic size can - 1/4 cups
No. 300 size can - 1 3/4 cups
No. 1 tall size can - 2 cups
No. 303 size can - 2 cups
No. 2 size can - 2 1/2 cups
No. 2 1/2 size can - 3 1/2 cups
No. 3 size can - 4 cups
No. 10 size can - 12 cups

## Measurements

4 tablespoons - 1/4 cup
5 1/2 tablespoons - 1/3 cup
8 tablespoons - 1/2 cup
3 teaspoon - 1 tablespoon
16 tablespoons - 1 cup
2 cups - 1 pint
2 pints - 1 quart
8 ounces - 1 cup
16 ounces - 1 pound
4 quarts liquid - 1 gallon
8 quarts solid - 1 peck
4 pecks - bushel
1 gallon - 128 ounces
1 quart - 32 ounces
1 pint - 16 ounces
1 cup - 8 ounces
1 teaspoon - 1/8 ounce
1 dash - 3 drops

## Oven Temperatures

Slow temperature - 300 degrees
Slow moderate temperature - 325 degrees
Moderate temperature - 350 degrees
Quick moderate temperature - 375 degrees
Moderate hot temperature - 400 degrees
Hot temperature - 425 degrees
Very hot temperature - 475 degrees

## Oven Baking Chart

These are typical baking times and usually will work if your recipe doesn't give the baking temperatures and times.

Biscuits - 450 for 12-15 minutes
Muffins - 400-425 for 20-25 minutes
Quick breads - 350 for 40-60 minutes
Yeast breads - 375-400 for 45-60 minutes
Yeast rolls - 400 for 25-20 minutes
Cupcakes - 375 for 20-25 minutes
Layer cakes - 350-375 for 25-35 minutes
Drop or rolled cookies - 350-375 for 8-12 minutes
Bar cookies - 350 for 25-30 minutes
Two crust pies - 450 for 10 minutes, then bake at
350 for 40 minutes

A true friend is one to whom
one may pour out all of the
contents of one's heart,
chaff and grain together,
knowing that the gentlest of hands
will take and sift it,
keep what is worth keeping
and, with the breath of kindness,
blow the rest away.

Arabian proverb

*Every cowboy or cowgirl needs a true friend, even if that friend is a horse.*

# WANTED

*Easy Way To Find Recipes*

## UNDERSTANDING COWS

PERHAPS NO LANGUAGE SYSTEM HAS BEEN HARDER FOR RESEARCHERS TO BREAK THAN THE HORN SIGNALS OF COWS. ALTHOUGH IN RECENT YEARS A FEW SIGNALS HAVE BEEN BROKEN. THEY ARE:

*v.t.* RIGHT TURN

*v.t.* LEFT TURN

*v.t.* STOP

1 *v.t.* CONFUSION, CHAOS; 2 *n.* a MAP, (ABOVE IS DETAILED DESCRIPTION OF A ROUTE TO INDIA)

1. *n.* LIGHTNING; 2. *n.* a GRAPH, (THIS ILLUS. IS OF RECENT CATTLE PRICES)

*pron. obj.,* ME
ME

NO FOOD

ZERO, NIL, EMPTY SET, NADA, ...

INFINITY

# *Appetizers and Beverages*

# *Breads*

## Main Dishes

### Casseroles

### Meats

## Candies

## Cookies

## Other Desserts

## Vegetables and Salads

## Miscellaneous

~~~~~~~~~~~~~~~~~~~~~~~~~~~~~~~~~~~~~~~~~~~~

## A Tip of a Hat to All of You

Thank you family (Jerry, Tracy, Travis, Mom, Dad, Hal and LeAnn) and friends who helped me get The Best Little Cookbook In The West to press! Thanks to Dave for offering to distribute the book, Duane for letting me use your equipment, plus Kay, Linda and Delaine for all your help. I want to thank Laura for the great cartoons and for being so easy to work with. If I wore a western hat, I'd tip it to all of you!

~~~~~~~~~~~~~~~~~~~~~~~~~~~~~~~~~~~~~~~~~~~~

*A hearty western slap on the back to those of you who shared your recipes, remedies and reminiscings with me, including:*

Jerry, Tracy and Travis
Dorothy Vaad
Edith Werner
Alvin Werner
Pat Blum
SD Cattlewomen and
SD Cowbelles'
    Red Beef Cookbook
Mary Liz Schlotte
Edna Gunderson
Linda Den Beste
Ruth Blum
Gertrude Harless
Matt Werner
LeAnn Werner
Geneva Krois
Octavia Den Beste
Jeanne Holst
Hal Werner
Delaine Ellis
Carol Boyd
Thunderstik Lodge
Sharon Weber
Bro. David Nagel
Father John Klingler
Brenda Allderdice
Jack Allderdice
Peggy Allderdice
Linda McFarland
Mary Haaland
Pat Haglund and her Mom
Josephine Schwenke
Alice Olson
Cheryl Jordan
Dori Gunderson
Dixie Thompson
Percie Blare
Neoma Rossow

S. Long
Scott Voorhis
Marcia Blecha
Kay Andera
Tim Thomas
Dina Brandt
Terry Hogan
Donna Dominiack
Agnes Ekstrum
Ron Schara
Timothy Burrell
Amber Renner
Lyla Erickson
Duke Warren
Marjean Warren
Dayle Blasius
Theresa Blasius
Kari Blasius
Jill Blasius
Darla Gray
Pennie Gill
Diane Sharping
Jim Blare
Margie Blare
Jay Blum
Hilda Fors
Velma Yates
John Blum
Don Fletcher
JoAnne Fletcher
Jen Chernock
Marcia Zeman
Trisha Burke
Rebecca Ellis
Sally Stewart
Donna Knippling
Rocky Knippling
Alice Nowicki

*Note: Fictitious names and characteristics have been given to many of the recipes and contributors. Any resemblance to people living or dead is purely coincidental!*

Notes:

## DAKOTA

My thoughts wander to the mountains
And then come back to the plain
My heart goes out to the seashore
And then it comes back again

With the hills and plains together
Where the rivers wind their way
I long to be in Dakota
Ere the passing of this day

Take me back to old Dakota
Where the sky and earth seem blended
Back to that glorious country
Where every heartache is mended

I have wandered far over the ocean
I have visited foreign lands
But I long for old Dakota
More than for desert sands

You may go to every large city
Across this large earth you may roam
But you'll not find a place sweeter
Than my old Dakota home

And when my roaming is over
Oh I long for that golden West
So take me back to Dakota
Where I can have Home and Rest

*This poem was written by my mother,*
*Edith Harless Werner, in 1925*
*when she was 12 years old.*

Notes:

O Great Spirit, whose voice I hear in the winds
And whose breath gives life to all the world, hear me.
I come before you, one of your many children.
I am small and weak.
I need your strength and wisdom.
Let me walk in beauty, and
My eyes behold the red and purple sunset.
Make my hands respect the things you have made,
My ears sharp to hear your voice.
Make me wise so that I may know
The things you have taught my people,
The lesson you have hidden in every leaf and rock.
I seek strength not to be superior to my brothers,
But to be able to fight my greatest enemy--myself.
Make me ever ready to come to you
With clean hands and straight eyes.
So when life fades as a fading sunset,
My spirit may come to you without shame.

Author Unknown